# EDNA ST. VINCENT MILLAY

# EDNA ST. VINCENT MILLAY

## CAROLYN DAFFRON

CHELSEA HOUSE PUBLISHERS

NEW YORK · PHILADELPHIA

All quotations from Edna St. Vincent Millay's poetry and let-
ters are reprinted by permission of Elizabeth Barnett, Literary
Executor for the Estate of Edna St. Vincent Millay/Norma
Millay Ellis.

**Chelsea House Publishers**
EDITOR-IN-CHIEF Nancy Toff
EXECUTIVE EDITOR Remmel T. Nunn
MANAGING EDITOR Karyn Gullen Browne
COPY CHIEF Juliann Barbato
PICTURE EDITOR Adrian G. Allen
ART DIRECTOR Maria Epes
MANUFACTURING MANAGER Gerald Levine

**American Women of Achievement**
SENIOR EDITOR Constance Jones

**Staff for EDNA ST. VINCENT MILLAY**
TEXT EDITOR Marian W. Taylor
DEPUTY COPY CHIEF Nicole Bowen
EDITORIAL ASSISTANT Claire Wilson
PICTURE RESEARCHERS Diana Gongora and Nisa Rauschenberg
ASSISTANT ART DIRECTOR Loraine Machlin
DESIGNER Donna Sinisgalli
LAYOUT Design Oasis
PRODUCTION COORDINATOR Joseph Romano
COVER ART Lisa Desimini
COVER ORNAMENT Loraine Machlin

First Printing
1  3  5  7  9  8  6  4  2

**Library of Congress Cataloging-in-Publication Data**

Daffron, Carolyn
  Edna St. Vincent Millay.

  (American women of achievement)
  Includes index.
1. Millay, Edna St. Vincent, 1892–1950—Juvenile
literature.   2. Authors, American—20th century—
Biography—Juvenile literature.   I. Title.   II. Series.
PS3525.I495Z63  1989      811'.52 [B]      88-35298
ISBN 1-55546-668-0
    0-7910-0444-9 (pbk.)

# CONTENTS

# AMERICAN WOMEN OF ACHIEVEMENT

**Abigail Adams**
*women's rights advocate*

**Jane Addams**
*social worker*

**Louisa May Alcott**
*author*

**Marian Anderson**
*singer*

**Susan B. Anthony**
*woman suffragist*

**Ethel Barrymore**
*actress*

**Clara Barton**
*founder of the American
Red Cross*

**Elizabeth Blackwell**
*physician*

**Nellie Bly**
*journalist*

**Margaret Bourke-White**
*photographer*

**Pearl Buck**
*author*

**Rachel Carson**
*biologist and author*

**Mary Cassatt**
*artist*

**Agnes De Mille**
*choreographer*

**Emily Dickinson**
*poet*

**Isadora Duncan**
*dancer*

**Amelia Earhart**
*aviator*

**Mary Baker Eddy**
*founder of the Christian
Science church*

**Betty Friedan**
*feminist*

**Althea Gibson**
*tennis champion*

**Emma Goldman**
*political activist*

**Helen Hayes**
*actress*

**Lillian Hellman**
*playwright*

**Katharine Hepburn**
*actress*

**Karen Horney**
*psychoanalyst*

**Anne Hutchinson**
*religious leader*

**Mahalia Jackson**
*gospel singer*

**Helen Keller**
*humanitarian*

**Jeane Kirkpatrick**
*diplomat*

**Emma Lazarus**
*poet*

**Clare Boothe Luce**
*author and diplomat*

**Barbara McClintock**
*biologist*

**Margaret Mead**
*anthropologist*

**Edna St. Vincent Millay**
*poet*

**Julia Morgan**
*architect*

**Grandma Moses**
*painter*

**Louise Nevelson**
*sculptor*

**Sandra Day O'Connor**
*Supreme Court justice*

**Georgia O'Keeffe**
*painter*

**Eleanor Roosevelt**
*diplomat and humanitarian*

**Wilma Rudolph**
*champion athlete*

**Florence Sabin**
*medical researcher*

**Beverly Sills**
*opera singer*

**Gertrude Stein**
*author*

**Gloria Steinem**
*feminist*

**Harriet Beecher Stowe**
*author and abolitionist*

**Mae West**
*entertainer*

**Edith Wharton**
*author*

**Phillis Wheatley**
*poet*

**Babe Didrikson Zaharias**
*champion athlete*

**CHELSEA HOUSE PUBLISHERS**

# "REMEMBER THE LADIES"

## MATINA S. HORNER

Remember the Ladies." That is what Abigail Adams wrote to her husband, John, then a delegate to the Continental Congress, as the Founding Fathers met in Philadelphia to form a new nation in March of 1776. "Be more generous and favorable to them than your ancestors. Do not put such unlimited power in the hands of the Husbands. If particular care and attention is not paid to the Ladies," Abigail Adams warned, "we are determined to foment a Rebellion, and will not hold ourselves bound by any Laws in which we have no voice, or Representation."

The words of Abigail Adams, one of the earliest American advocates of women's rights, were prophetic. Because when we have not "remembered the ladies," they have, by their words and deeds, reminded us so forcefully of the omission that we cannot fail to remember them. For the history of American women is as interesting and varied as the history of our nation as a whole. American women have played an integral part in founding, settling, and building our country. Some we remember as remarkable women who—against great odds—achieved distinction in the public arena: Anne Hutchinson, who in the 17th century became a charismatic religious leader; Phillis Wheatley, an 18th-century black slave who became a poet; Susan B. Anthony, whose name is synonymous with the 19th-century women's rights movement and who led the struggle to enfranchise women; and, in our own century, Amelia Earhart, the first woman to cross the Atlantic Ocean by air.

7

These extraordinary women certainly merit our admiration, but other women, "common women," many of them all but forgotten, should also be recognized for their contributions to American thought and culture. Women have been community builders; they have founded schools and formed voluntary associations to help those in need; they have assumed the major responsibility for rearing children, passing on from one generation to the next the values that keep a culture alive. These and innumerable other contributions, once ignored, are now being recognized by scholars, students, and the public. It is exciting and gratifying to realize that a part of our history that was hardly acknowledged a few generations ago is now being studied and brought to light.

In recent decades, the field of women's history has grown from obscurity to a politically controversial splinter movement to academic respectability, in many cases mainstreamed into such traditional disciplines as history, economics, and psychology. Scholars of women, both female and male, have organized research centers at such prestigious institutions as Wellesley College, Stanford University, and the University of California. Other notable centers for women's studies are the Center for the American Woman and Politics at the Eagleton Institute of Politics at Rutgers University; the Henry A. Murray Research Center for the Study of Lives, at Radcliffe College; and the Women's Research and Education Institute, the research arm of the Congressional Caucus on Women's Issues. Other scholars and public figures have established archives and libraries, such as the Schlesinger Library on the History of Women in America, at Radcliffe College, and the Sophia Smith Collection, at Smith College, to collect and preserve the written and tangible legacies of women.

From the initial donation of the Women's Rights Collection in 1943, the Schlesinger Library grew to encompass vast collections documenting the manifold accomplishments of American women. Simultaneously, the women's movement in general and the academic discipline of women's studies in particular also began with a narrow definition and gradually expanded their mandate. Early causes such as woman suffrage and social reform, abolition and organized labor were joined by newer concerns such as the history of women in business and the professions and in politics and government; the study of the family; and social issues such as health policy and education.

Women, as historian Arthur M. Schlesinger, jr., once pointed out, "have constituted the most spectacular casualty of traditional history.

They have made up at least half the human race, but you could never tell that by looking at the books historians write.'' The new breed of historians is remedying that omission. They have written books about immigrant women and about working-class women who struggled for survival in cities and about black women who met the challenges of life in rural areas. They are telling the stories of women who, despite the barriers of tradition and economics, became lawyers and doctors and public figures.

The women's studies movement has also led scholars to question traditional interpretations of their respective disciplines. For example, the study of war has traditionally been an exercise in military and political analysis, an examination of strategies planned and executed by men. But scholars of women's history have pointed out that wars have also been periods of tremendous change and even opportunity for women, because the very absence of men on the home front enabled them to expand their educational, economic, and professional activities and to assume leadership in their homes.

The early scholars of women's history showed a unique brand of courage in choosing to investigate new subjects and take new approaches to old ones. Often, like their subjects, they endured criticism and even ostracism by their academic colleagues. But their efforts have unquestionably been worthwhile, because with the publication of each new study and book another piece of the historical patchwork is sewn into place, revealing an increasingly comprehensive picture of the role of women in our rich and varied history.

Such books on groups of women are essential, but books that focus on the lives of individuals are equally indispensable. Biographies can be inspirational, offering their readers the example of people with vision who have looked outside themselves for their goals and have often struggled against great obstacles to achieve them. Marian Anderson, for instance, had to overcome racial bigotry in order to perfect her art and perform as a concert singer. Isadora Duncan defied the rules of classical dance to find true artistic freedom. Jane Addams had to break down society's notions of the proper role for women in order to create new social institutions, notably the settlement house. All of these women had to come to terms both with themselves and with the world in which they lived. Only then could they move ahead as pioneers in their chosen callings.

Biography can inspire not only by adulation but also by realism. It helps us to see not only the qualities in others that we hope to emulate but also, perhaps, the weaknesses that made them "human." By helping us identify with the subject on a more personal level they help us to feel that we, too, can achieve such goals. We read about Eleanor Roosevelt, for example, who occupied a unique and seemingly enviable position as the wife of the president. Yet we can sympathize with her inner dilemma: an inherently shy woman who had to force herself to live a most public life in order to use her position to benefit others. We may not be able to imagine ourselves having the immense poetic talent of Emily Dickinson, but from her story we can understand the challenges faced by a creative woman who was expected to fulfill many family responsibilities. And though few of us will ever reach the level of athletic accomplishment displayed by Wilma Rudolph or Babe Zaharias, we can still appreciate their spirit, their overwhelming will to excel.

A biography is a multifaceted lens. It is first of all a magnification, the intimate examination of one particular life. But at the same time, it is a wide-angle lens, informing us about the world in which the subject lived. We come away from reading about one life knowing more about the social, political, and economic fabric of the time. It is for this reason, perhaps, that the great New England essayist Ralph Waldo Emerson wrote, in 1841, "There is properly no history: only biography." And it is also why biography, and particularly women's biography, will continue to fascinate writers and readers alike.

# EDNA ST. VINCENT MILLAY

*Auburn-haired, green-eyed, and tiny, 20-year-old poet Edna St. Vincent Millay of Camden, Maine, was often described as "elfinlike."*

# ONE

# "Renascence"

Edna St. Vincent Millay reached a turning point in her life in 1912, when she was 20 years old. She had graduated from high school in Camden, Maine, in 1909, praised for her intelligence, her quick wit, and her musical and literary gifts. She had been optimistic and eager to conquer the world's challenges, but three years later, she had yet to meet them. Life in Camden was pleasant enough: Millay enjoyed living at home with her mother and two sisters, and she took constant delight in the hills and rugged seacoast around Camden, where she had spent most of her life since her parents' divorce in 1900. Still, she felt restless, hemmed in by her small-town existence, impatient for her adult life to begin.

Millay did, however, have plenty to keep her busy. Her mother, a visiting practical nurse, was often away; while she attended to her cases, Millay cooked and ran the household for her younger sisters, Norma and Kathleen. She also worked as a stenographer and typist for summer tourists, occasionally acted in amateur and stock-company plays, and took an active part in several social clubs for young women. When she was alone, she climbed the steep mountains around Camden, picked blueberries on the gentler hills, and walked along the shores of the Atlantic Ocean and nearby Lake Megunticook. At home, she loved to play the piano and compose songs. But what she enjoyed most was writing poetry; she had been expressing her feelings through poems since she was five years old.

By the time Millay reached 14, she was a published author: Her poems had appeared not only in her high school

*Camden's surroundings include serene Lake Megunticook (above),*

magazine, *The Megunticook*, but in *St. Nicholas Magazine*, a national periodical aimed at young readers. *Saint Nicholas*, however, accepted writing only from people under the age of 18. When she passed that age, she had no idea how to get her work published, but she kept on writing poetry.

One long poem, which came to be called "Renascence," reflected the sentiments that preoccupied her late teenage years. She began writing it in 1910, when she was 18. She was still working on it in the early spring of 1912, when she received a letter from her father, who was then living in Kingman, Maine, about 100 miles north of Camden. Although Cora Millay and her daughters had seen little of Henry Millay in recent years, they had remained on good terms after the 1900 divorce. When Henry wrote to say he was ill with pneumonia and would welcome the company of his eldest daughter, Edna Millay quickly agreed to join him.

*the inspiration for several of Millay's early poems.*

While Millay was in Kingman, her mother was also away from home, working on a nursing assignment. As Cora Millay sat by her sleeping patient's bedside one night, she began leafing through a discarded magazine; in it, she found an intriguing announcement. It invited American poets to send their work to *The Lyric Year*, a new poetry anthology that would include the 100 best poems submitted. The three top poems would be awarded cash prizes, one of $500 and two of $250

each. Cora Millay, whose faith in her daughter's poetic talent was boundless, wrote Edna the next morning, urging her to hurry home and prepare her poetry for submission to the contest. Edna Millay returned to Camden almost at once (her father was on the mend), put the finishing touches on "Renascence," and sent it to *The Lyric Year*. She waited for a response in a fever of anticipation.

*The Lyric Year* contest caused enormous excitement among American poets, who—then as now—had few outlets for their poems and very little chance of earning money by writing poetry. More than 10,000 entries arrived at the office of the anthology's editor, Ferdinand Earle. Fortunately for Millay, she had no way of knowing how many poets were vying for publication or how close her own entry came to being discarded as laughably bad.

"Piles of disgustingly awful *rot* ... was submitted to me as poetry," Earle later wrote. Nevertheless, he and a friend, Professor Montague Donner, equipped themselves with a pair of tall wastebaskets and settled in to examine manuscripts. According to Earle, most of them were "insipid and driveling nonsense" and went right into the baskets.

Describing the scene in a letter to an associate, Earle recalled that at one point he heard Donner chuckling as he threw his latest reject away. "What's so amusing?" he asked. Still laughing, Donner retrieved a long envelope from his basket and began to read a poem:

All I could see from where I stood
Was three long mountains and a wood;
I turned and looked another way,
And saw three islands in a bay.

The simplicity of these lines misled Donner into thinking that the poem was trite, even childish. Still chuckling with derision, he threw the submission back into the wastebasket. But Earle, he recalled, said, "Hey! That sounds good!" and made his friend fish out the manuscript yet again. This time Donner read the poem's final stanza, which begins:

The world stands out on either side
No wider than the heart is wide;
Above the world is stretched the sky,—
No higher than the soul is high.

"It doesn't sound so bad after all!" Donner admitted. With growing admiration, he read the whole poem aloud, all 10 pages of it. When he had finished, the two men were so struck by its beauty and originality that Donner read it aloud again. "We both agreed it was tops," recalled Earle.

"Renascence" tells the story of the narrator's symbolic death and rebirth. When the poem begins, the narrator feels "bounded" by the world around her: No matter where she turns, she sees the same landscape, the same "three long mountains and a wood." Her world appears small, stifling, claustrophobic. It seems to close in on her: She screams when she finds that the sky is so low she can lift her hand and touch it. Worse still, it is as if the whole weight of "Infinity," all the guilt and suffering in the world, is pressing against her.

The narrator wants only death, and she appears to get her wish. At first she is "gladly dead," thankful to be at rest six feet under the ground. But then rain begins to fall on the grave, and the poet remembers the glories of nature. She cries out to God to give her "new birth" so that she can "kiss the fingers of the rain" and "catch the freshened, fragrant breeze / From drenched and dripping apple-trees."

*Wearing identical outfits, Millay (right) and a fellow high school graduate join an older friend for a commencement-day snapshot in 1909.*

*The Camden of 1912 (above) was an easygoing, pleasant town, but to a restless young poet, it seemed narrow and stifling.*

Her prayer is answered. The rain becomes a torrent and washes over her. She can see and hear the world again; she can smell "a miracle of orchard-breath." She springs from the ground, radiant with joy and aware, at last, that nature is her salvation: "God, I can push the grass apart / And lay my finger on Thy heart!"

The poem ends with a summing-up of what the narrator has learned:

The heart can push the sea and land
Farther away on either hand;
The soul can split the sky in two,
And let the face of God shine through.
But East and West will pinch the heart
That can not keep them pushed apart;
And he whose soul is flat—the sky
Will cave in on him by and by.

Some themes in "Renascence" grew out of Millay's own life. Like the po-em's narrator, Millay passionately loved nature. And she too felt increasingly trapped by circumstance, by the life of a young, rather poor woman in a small town in coastal Maine.

When he first heard and marveled at her poetry, Ferdinand Earle had no idea that Millay was so young or that she had lived so sheltered a life. From its polish and wisdom, he assumed that "Renascence" was the work of a much older writer. Because she had signed her poem "E. St. Vincent Millay," as was her custom, he also assumed that Millay was a man. Without consulting his two fellow contest judges, Earle sent off a letter to "E. St. Vincent Millay, Esq., Dear Sir: . . . " He told her how much he admired "Renascence" and said he was confident that the

18

*Millay (seated, third from left) enjoys a summer outing with friends. Swimming and sailing parties were favorite pastimes of Camden's young people.*

poem would win the $500 first prize.

Millay must have been ecstatic when she got the letter. Winning first prize in the *Lyric Year* contest would have meant recognition and appreciation beyond her wildest hopes. And for a struggling family in 1912, $500 was a fabulous sum, equal to more than $5,000 in today's currency.

But in his enthusiasm, Earle had spoken too soon. Although they liked the poem, neither of the other two judges thought "Renascence" should get any prize at all, much less the first. It was all Earle could do to persuade *The Lyric Year* to award "Renascence" fourth place, which carried no cash award. This news undoubtedly disappointed the Millays, but the publication of "Renascence" would change Edna St. Vincent Millay's life—and American literature—forever.

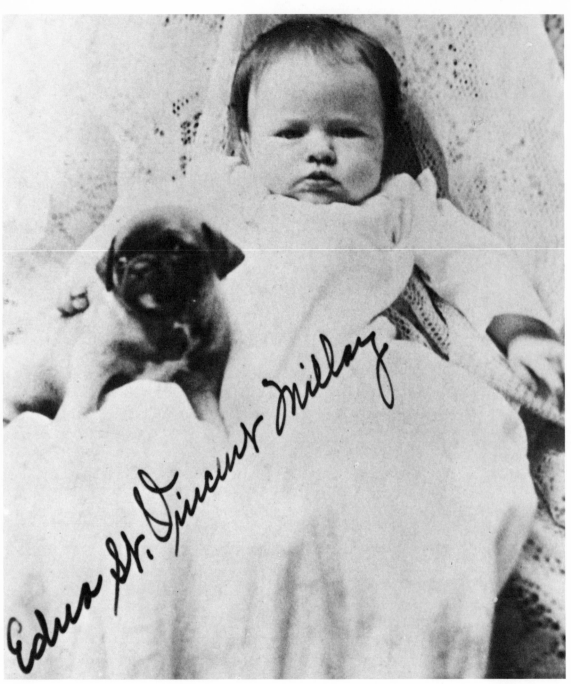

*As an adult, Edna St. Vincent Millay autographed this copy of her first portrait, made in Rockland, Maine, in early 1892.*

# TWO

# Queen of the Dishpans

Edna St. Vincent Millay was born to Henry and Cora Buzzelle Millay on February 22, 1892, in the small town of Rockland, Maine. She owed her unusual middle name to a series of events that took place just before she was born: Her mother's young sailor brother, seriously injured during a storm at sea, had been nursed back to health at St. Vincent's Hospital in New York City; to show her appreciation, Cora Millay named her daughter for the institution.

Millay went by various names at different stages of her life. She was Vincent to relatives and friends during her childhood and Edna to those who met her as an adult. And when she submitted her childhood poetry to magazines, she used the name E. St. Vincent Millay.

Soon after Vincent's birth the Millays moved to Union, another small Maine town, where Henry Millay worked as a high school teacher and administrator. In Union, a second Millay daughter, golden-haired Norma, was born in late 1893; dark-haired Kathleen, the Millays' third and last child, arrived three years later.

A talented singer and pianist, Cora Millay passionately loved music and literature. But her husband—intelligent, good-looking, and popular Henry Millay—apparently preferred poker to piano playing. Cora Millay, who was determined to nurture any artistic gifts her three daughters might have, hated to see money gambled away when it could have been spent on the children. As the years passed, Henry's constant gambling and Cora's constant disap-

*Edna's father, Henry Tolman Millay (above), was popular with his neighbors and colleagues, but his addiction to gambling destroyed his marriage.*

After his wife divorced him, Henry Millay was more like a kindly, somewhat distant uncle to the girls than a father. He kept in touch with his daughters, followed their successes with pride, sent them money for special occasions if they wrote him for it, and remained on friendly terms with their mother. But he never again lived in the same town as his children, gave them regular financial support, or took part in their rearing. The three girls rarely saw him while they were growing up.

The Millay women rarely spoke about Henry Millay or about the divorce. Years afterward, in fact, a close friend of Edna St. Vincent Millay said the poet mentioned her father to him only once in her entire adult life. But a letter from Vincent Millay, sent to her family while she was nursing her father in Kingman, shows that she treasured his affection and that she was proud of him: "I see Papa twice a day. We can't talk very much, but he loves to have me with him. . . . I never heard so many people inquire for one man. All festivities are postponed until he recovers. An M.D. and an L.L.D. [a lawyer] from somewhere around here came on the train today just to see him a minute—great friends of his."

proval created increasing strain on their marriage. Finally, Cora Millay decided she could no longer stand her husband's irresponsible ways.

As an adult, Edna St. Vincent Millay would recall one very sad day: "I remember a swamp," she wrote, "when I was seven. It was down across that swamp that my father went, when my mother told him to go & not come back. (Or maybe she said he might come back if he would do better—but who ever does better?)"

For three years after the divorce, Cora Millay and her daughters boarded with relatives, moving from one small town to another. In 1903, the family settled into a small rented house in Camden, and there they stayed until the girls grew up. Cora supported them by working as a practical nurse, taking care of invalids in their homes. At first she worked only at night so she could be with the girls during the day. In her spare moments she supplemented her meager nurse's wages by making false hairpieces, then highly fashionable. When Vincent was about 12, Cora Millay began taking cases that paid more but that required daytime or even round-the-clock nursing, often in another town. Sometimes a job kept her away from home for days or even weeks at a stretch.

Like most rural Americans of the time, the Millays lighted their house with oil lamps and heated it with wood fires. When Cora Millay was away on a

*The seacoast town of Camden, seen here in a photograph from the late 1800s, was home to the three Millay sisters during most of their school-age years.*

*Cora Buzzelle Millay, mother of Edna, Norma, and Kathleen, supported her daughters as a practical nurse after she divorced her husband.*

family love. Her childhood, she told a friend many years later, had been "extraordinarily happy." To another friend, she said, "it never rained in those days." Whatever the Millay children thought of their father, they never showed the slightest doubt that their mother loved, understood, and admired them. Aware that she hated to be separated from them, they were proud of her and grateful for the hard work she did for them.

Cora Millay made all the girls' clothes, and when she was at home between cases, she tried to do at least a week's worth of baking and laundry. But, most important in the eyes of both mother and daughters, Cora Millay took the time to see to her girls' cultural education. She made sure they learned about literature, music, art, and nature. When she found herself with a bit of extra money, she bought a small portable organ, on which she and her eldest daughter played and composed hundreds of songs. Out of her slender purse, she somehow produced enough money for concert tickets, music lessons, and magazine subscriptions. She also helped promote classical music in Camden by playing piano with the town orchestra and writing out its musical scores.

case, it was up to her daughters to see that the wood was chopped, the fire lit and tended, the lamps trimmed, the water for washing heated over burning wood. During the cold Maine winters, just keeping the house warm could be a full-time job.

Although the Millay girls grew up with no father; an often absent, overworked mother; many responsibilities; and very little money, most accounts of Vincent Millay's youth describe it as a time of joy, high spirits, security, and

Although her family sometimes did without a few of life's necessities, Edna Millay once recalled, they rarely lacked for its luxuries. They all agreed, for example, that one could exist with very little heat, but that books were a must. Cora Millay acquired every book—poetry, novels, plays, musical biographies, nature textbooks, encyclo-pedias—she could lay hands on. Talk-ing to an interviewer about her daugh-ters many years later, she said, "So strong in me was the belief in them and their future that, no matter how hard it was, I had to have . . . books—I had the best private library in Camden—everything that would contribute to their development." Cora Millay firmly believed that her girls were ex-ceptional, capable of doing great things if they worked hard enough. (And, in-deed, all three did make their mark on the world. Kathleen wrote fiction; Norma became an actress and opera singer.) They all credited their mother with inspiring them. "Everything I did you encouraged," said the adult Edna in a letter to her mother. "I can not remember once in my life when you were not interested in what I was work-ing on, or even suggested that I should put it aside for something else."

The Millays' Camden neighbors must have shaken their heads over the way Cora Millay let her girls run wild, free of any consistent adult authority. It is true that Vincent, Norma, and Kathleen were allowed far more free-dom than was customary in those days, or even in many families today. Of course, unless she gave up her much-needed job, Cora Millay had no choice but to leave her girls at home, with Vincent in charge. But Cora Millay also believed that freedom and responsibil-ity should begin early and—a radical notion at the time—that girls should have the same amount of freedom and privacy as boys. She trusted her chil-

dren to take care of the house and each other while she was away, and she trusted them never to deceive her.

Happily for all concerned, the moth-er's views about housekeeping and do-mestic routines were as unorthodox as her daughters'. It never bothered Cora Millay to learn that the girls had let the dishes pile up, preferring to sing around the piano after dinner, or act out plays together, before falling into bed. When all the plates in the house were dirty, Vincent would organize a marathon clean-up session. The Millay girls made dishwashing, like most of their chores, into a game. Vincent even wrote special songs to wash dishes by. One of them was called "I'm the Queen of the Dish-pans":

> There are pots and pans and kettles
>   galore;
> When I think I'm all done there's
>   always some more:
> For here's a dozen and there's a score,
> I'm the Queen of the Dishpans—
>   hooray!

It was the same with general house-keeping. The girls liked to have the house scrubbed and tidy for their moth-er's return. They knew she would not be angry about dirt and disorder, but they also knew she would do whatever work needed doing, no matter how tired she was. When the time came to tackle a room, Vincent would shout, "Corner!" Each of the three sisters would then dash to a corner of the room and start cleaning at breakneck speed. They worked toward the middle and did the fourth corner together. With luck, and depending on the sea-son, they would still have time to run up the hill for blueberries, or down to the bog for cranberries, or out to the bay for a swim, or into the snow to have fun with their friends.

Like their mother, the Millay girls had a gift for making the best of things. One winter morning, for example, Vincent and her sisters awoke to discover that the water pipes had burst and flooded the kitchen floor. Because there was no heat, the water had frozen all across the floor. The girls' immediate response was to put on their ice skates and take advantage of Camden's first indoor rink.

The Millay girls also went to bed whenever they pleased, which was often much later than the bedtimes of the other local girls. One of Vincent's high school friends wrote about a late-night visit to the Millay house. Vincent, she recalled, was wearing a full skirt that brushed the tops of her high-button boots, a belt that "circumscribed a wide equator around her tiny middle," and a white muslin blouse with a lace-edged collar. "A wide blue bow," continued the friend, "spread its wings behind her head where her reddish-gold hair was fastened in a 'bun.'"

Books were piled on the floor. In the center of the table, which had been cleared for card playing, was a plate of warm fudge. The girls—there were a half-dozen at the house that night—played cards, sang popular songs, and lost track of the time. When the clock struck 12:00, one girl cried: "What will my mother say?" But they could not bear to leave, and Vincent could not

*A canoe rests on the shore of Lake Megunticook, one of young Edna Millay's favorite spots. The poet and her friends often boated on the wide, clear lake.*

bear to see them go until they had sung a few more songs. When they left, she was standing in the doorway, still singing. Her clear voice followed them down the hill: "Adieu, adieu, kind friends, adieu."

After Edna St. Vincent Millay had become famous, her more distant acquaintances from Camden days— especially the boys—remembered her as a plain, quiet girl who never seemed to care about anything except nature. Closer friends remembered her quite differently, as a girl whose "feet were light in the dance," whose voice was "rollicking and gay when the crowd gathered for a sing."

*Millay, who liked to adorn her reddish-gold hair with ribbons, wears a pair of huge bows for her high school graduation picture in 1909.*

*Extremely popular with other girls in high school, Millay was less well liked by the boys; she was, said one male schoolmate, "too smart for most of us."*

# THREE

# Early Inspirations

One bird on a tree,
One bird come to me.
One bird on the ground,
One bird hopping round.
One bird in his nest,
One bird took a rest.

This is Edna St. Vincent Millay's first poem, or at least the first one anyone wrote down. It is not, perhaps, immortal verse—but, then, the poet was only about five years old when she composed it. A few years later, "One Bird" became the first entry in a little brown notebook labeled *Poetical Works of E. Vincent Millay* and dedicated in a scratchy scrawl to "my mother, whose interest and understanding have been the life of many of These Works, and the Inspiration of many more."

If Cora Millay ever smiled at her daughter's grand words and poetic flights, she must have done so in private. From the first, she took Vincent's poems seriously and treated her daughter's creative talent with complete re-

spect. Cora Millay was a writer herself. When she could find time, she wrote poems and short stories, some of which were printed in local newspapers and regional magazines. After her girls had grown up, she published *Little Otis*, a full-length book of children's poetry. Vincent was raised in a household where writing a poem was considered as normal as cooking a meal or scrubbing a floor—and far more important.

As biographer Miriam Gurko points out in *Restless Spirit: The Life of Edna St. Vincent Millay*, the intellectual climate of that era also favored poetry: "Writing, even the writing of poetry, and certainly the reading and recitation of poetry, were far more natural than they would be in later decades. Girls took elocution lessons, and recited poems as part of an evening's entertainment. . . . People quoted poetry with no self-consciousness or sense of affectation; they wrote it with equal directness."

Vincent found her greatest early inspiration in nature. The young poet was fortunate to grow up on one of the most beautiful stretches of seacoast in America. The busy harbor town of Camden was rimmed with orchards, meadows, and berry patches. To the north, rising dramatically above the

town, was Mount Battie, from the summit of which Vincent saw the panoramic view that inspired "Renascence." She loved to climb the steep slope and look down on Penobscot Bay, with its small, jewellike islands, or across the water to the hills in the north and west.

When she was growing up, Vincent often joined her friends on canoe trips, swimming parties, and hikes. She enjoyed these activities, but what she liked best was spending time alone in

the woods and meadows near Camden. As she later described herself, the young poet was "earth-ecstatic," finding in nature a sublime, almost religious inspiration. The songs of the spring warblers filled her with wild joy. The sight of a newborn fawn walking among tall ferns, its eyes looking out "with mild, attracted, wondering gaze," made her feel a thrill of rapture, as if the world had been newly made that morning.

Vincent also spent countless hours

reading, especially during the long, cold Maine winters. By the time she was seven, she was reading great literature on her own—not because she felt she should, but because she liked it. She read, and often memorized, works by the classical English poets; her favorites were John Milton, William Wordsworth, and Percy Bysshe Shelley. By the time she was nine years old, she had read most of Shakespeare's plays and poems, and she began reading Latin poetry in elementary school. She loved the sound of Latin. For the rest of her life, she read Latin love poems when she wanted to relax.

Vincent wrote poetry throughout her childhood. In 1905, when she was 13, she joined the St. Nicholas League, an organization for aspiring writers under the age of 18. The league was sponsored by *St. Nicholas*, a young people's magazine that included a section every month for its subscribers' creative writing.

In 1906, "Forest Trees"—Millay's first published poem—appeared in the October issue of *St. Nicholas*. During the next few years, the magazine published five more of Vincent's poems. One of them, "The Land of Romance," received the league's coveted Gold Badge and was later republished in *Current Literature*, a magazine for adults. Calling the poem "phenomenal," the *Current Literature* editors

*A photograph taken from Mount Battie shows Camden's shoreline. It was this view that Millay described in her poem "Renascence."*

31

*A fawn and its mother graze in a New England forest. "Earth-ecstatic," Millay spent many childhood hours exploring the woods and fields around Camden.*

marveled that "its author (whether boy or girl, we do not know) is only 14 years of age."

"Friends," the last poem Vincent sent *St. Nicholas*, shortly before she turned 18, won the magazine's highest award—$5 in cash. She used the money to buy a volume of Robert Browning's poetry. In a thank-you letter to the editors, she said she admired Browning

so much that "my prize will give me more pleasure in that form than in any other." Her letter closed on a wistful note: "I am sorry to grow up and leave you."

Vincent attended the local public schools in Camden. A good student in grammar school, she skipped part of eighth grade. At Camden High School, she was brilliant in languages, good in most other subjects, and terrible in algebra. Her teachers generally liked her, despite what one school friend recalled as "her exasperating tendency to question and probe during classroom discussions." And she was extremely popular with her female classmates, who often congregated at the Millay house on winter evenings to do homework together. Millay would help her friends with English, Latin, and French; they would help her with algebra and sometimes pitch in with the housekeeping as well.

Often, a group of girls would stay for dinner, but if Cora Millay was away on a case, guests never knew what they would get to eat. "The first time I was invited to supper," one of Vincent's schoolmates recalled, "Vincent vaguely produced a date pie from the bakery—and nothing else. I was hungry, so I offered to make potato stew as a first course." The Millay girls extravagantly praised their friend's concoction, a mixture of milk, potatoes, and salt pork, often called "poor man's stew."

From then on, Vincent's friend made poor man's stew whenever she visited the Millay girls. "My mother used to ask me why I liked washing dishes and making potato stew at the Millays' when I hated to do those things at home," recalled the friend. "It was because Vincent made everything wonderful fun ... but she would never discuss people, and wouldn't listen if others did, and she could be a spitfire if she thought something wasn't fair. No one ever heard a word of gossip from Vincent, or a swear word—not even slang."

The girls adored Vincent, but the boys were another matter. Norma and Kathleen—who, some recall, were both more conventionally pretty than their sister in those days—had many male admirers. But except for one fairly close platonic (nonromantic) friend, young men showed no interest in the oldest Millay girl, except when they became downright hostile to her. Looking back on his high school days some 50 years later, one of her male classmates wrote:

"I remember Vincent as a scrawny girl—not nearly as attractive as her pretty sister, Norma—and too smart for most of us. . . . She hadn't learned—as many brilliant women do—to hide her superior gifts from young male clods." Perhaps increasing Vincent's unpopularity with Camden's young men was the fact that she rarely paid them the slightest attention.

Vincent took an active part in high school literary life. She contributed essays and poems to the school publication, *The Megunticook* and, in her senior year, served as the paper's editor in chief. But when it came time to elect the class poet at graduation, the boys in her class, who outnumbered the girls, got together and elected a boy.

Vincent, who had already started writing the class poem, was bitterly disappointed, but she finished the verses and submitted them as her re-

*When Millay recited her poetry at Camden's Whitehall Inn (below) in 1912, one listener was so impressed that she offered to help send the young woman to college.*

quired senior essay. The poem, "La Joie de Vivre" (the joy of living, in French), won the school's first prize for a senior essay and received ringing applause when she read it at her graduation ceremony in June 1909. "La Joie de Vivre" recounts Vincent's delight in being young and alive. Among its lines are these:

> I will not miss
> One joy from out the living. I will go
> Through valleys low, where deep-set
>   mountains throw
> A shadow and a shelter from the
>   heat. . .
> Deep draw I in my breath,
> Deep drink of water cold;
> There is no growing old,

*Poet Arthur Davison Ficke (below), who read Millay's "Renascence" in 1912, at first refused to believe the poem had been written by "some sweet young thing of 20."*

> There is no death.
> The world and I are young!
> Never on lips of man,
> Never since time began,
> Has gladder song been sung.

Despite her male classmates' collusion, nobody in Camden doubted that Vincent was the most promising poet in the area. She also showed some theatrical talent: She wrote a school play, appeared in a number of local amateur productions, and played several small roles in plays staged by professional touring companies. Vincent thought she might have a future on the stage, and she was right. But she knew that acting would never hold the highest place in her heart.

Music was another matter. Vincent was a serious pianist, and for a while she seriously considered pursuing a concert career. Cora Millay had eventually replaced the family's small portable organ with a real piano, and Vincent had taken piano lessons for several years. When she was 12 years old, she went to visit her mother, who was working at the home of musician John Wheeler Tufts, a distinguished composer and retired music professor. While she was waiting in the parlor for her mother, Vincent caught sight of Tufts' grand piano. She could not resist: She tried out a few keys, then sat down and began playing a lively composition she had written herself. Her mother was shocked, but according to local legend, Tufts came running into the room shouting, "Bravo! Encore!"

When Tufts offered to teach Vincent without fee, Cora Millay happily

*Millay takes the helm of a friend's sailboat during a 1912 cruise off the Maine coast. The poet, who loved the ocean, often used it as an image in her work.*

agreed. Vincent was an apt pupil, and for the next few years, she and her teacher had hopes that she might become a piano soloist. The prospect dwindled as Vincent grew into adulthood, partly because her hands stayed the size of a young child's. Vincent even considered surgery to increase her handspan but finally discarded this idea and turned more and more to her poetry.

Edna St. Vincent Millay continued to play the piano, sometimes for hours each day. For the rest of her life, music remained one of the most intense joys of her existence. "Indeed, without music I should wish to die," she wrote when she was in her twenties. "Even poetry, sweet patron Muse forgive me the words, is not what music is."

Vincent also loved the water. From a very early age, she was drawn to the ocean, often perching alone on the rocks, watching the waves pound the beach, listening to the mournful cries of the circling gulls. One summer afternoon, she saw what she thought was a little green island a few hundred yards out to sea. She decided to swim to it. The island was much farther away than she thought, and her arms began to tire. Vincent pressed on: She could always rest once she reached the island. But when she got to its edge, she found not land, but a glistening mass of seaweed floating and winding in the seawater.

Recollections of that moment—her terror of drowning, her near panic at the feel of those slippery weeds, and her fierce determination to fight and live—stayed with her forever. When she finally made it back to shore, she collapsed on the sand, utterly exhausted. Some critics believe that this brush with death had a lasting effect on the poet's emotions, and that it inspired the intense death and rebirth imagery first seen in "Renascence."

*Intense* is the word most often used to describe the young Vincent Millay. She never loved, hated, worked, or played without completely committing herself. Where another young woman might be happy or sad, she was ecstatic or agonized. Wildly passionate and tremendously gifted, she felt increasingly stifled by her life in Camden. She longed to know the world beyond. Her wish would soon be granted.

In the summer of 1912, some two months before "Renascence" appeared in *The Lyric Year*, the Whitehall Inn, a Camden resort hotel, staged a talent show for its guests and employees. Norma Millay, who was working as a waitress at the inn, invited her sister Edna to come to the show; the pair turned out to be the stars of the evening. Norma won a prize for her dancing and Edna received enthusiastic applause when she played the piano, sang, and recited some light verse she had written.

Her listeners begged for more. After some hesitation, Millay sat down on a piano stool on the inn's long, shady porch and, in her soft, lilting voice, recited "Renascence" straight through. One of the enthralled listeners was Caroline Dow, head of the YWCA National Training School in New York City. Deeply impressed by the young poet's work, Dow asked about her plans for the future. When she discovered that Millay had nothing specific in mind, Dow urged her to apply for a college scholarship. She would, she told Millay, help her investigate colleges, arrange interviews, and find grants. Millay accepted Dow's offer with joy and began reading up on colleges to decide which one she preferred.

When *The Lyric Year* was published the following November, "Renascence" received more critical and popular acclaim than any other poem in the book. It was so well liked, in fact, that the judges' failure to award it a top prize caused a heated controversy in literary circles. The first-prize winner, Orrick Johns, later wrote that "when the book arrived, I realized that it was

*New Yorkers cross Broadway in the early 1920s. Millay described Manhattan as "buildings everywhere, seven and eight stories to million and billion stories."*

*The celebrated poet Sara Teasdale (above) was one of Millay's earliest fans. "When I first read you," she wrote Millay, "I knew you and named a star."*

an unmerited award. The outstanding poem in the book was 'Renascence' by Edna St. Vincent Millay, immediately recognized by every authoritative critic as such. The award was as much an embarrassment to me as a triumph." As one observer put it, Millay "became famous through *not* receiving the prize."

It was a heady time for Millay. A few months earlier she had been unknown, virtually unpublished, and totally unsure how she could pursue her creative life in Camden. Now she had national fame and, even more important to her, the respect of many poets and discriminating readers.

Among the established poets who wrote to her were Witter Bynner and Arthur Davison Ficke, who would become her lifelong friends. At first, Ficke and Bynner thought the authorship of "Renascence" was a hoax. The real author, they wrote to Earle, had to be "a brawny male of 45," not "some sweet young thing of 20." Millay responded with a letter and a photograph of herself. "The brawny male sends his picture," she wrote. "I *have* to laugh." These letters were the first of many that would be exchanged among Millay, Ficke, and Bynner over the years.

By February 1913 the "sweet young thing" was in New York City, taking courses at Barnard College to help prepare for Vassar College's entrance exams the following fall. She had decided on Vassar, she told her mother, because the college had "four girls from Persia, two from Syria, two from Japan . . .

*Framed by Washington Square's arch, tourists ride a Manhattan sightseeing bus. With Sara Teasdale, Millay explored the city on a similar vehicle in 1913.*

At the age of 21, Edna St. Vincent Millay felt her life was beginning at last. "I don't know where I'm going," she told her mother, "but I'm on my way."

There isn't one 'furriner' at Smith." Millay was determined to expand her horizons.

While she was in New York, Millay lived at the residence of the YWCA National Training School, where Caroline Dow helped her adjust to a much faster-paced life than she had ever known. "From my window in the daytime," Millay wrote home, "I can see *everything*—just buildings, tho, it is buildings everywhere, seven and eight stories to million and billion stories, washing drying on the roofs and on lines strung between the houses . . . and *noise*, yes, in New York you can *see* the noise."

Millay did not mind the noise a bit: "I can sleep better for it," she said. Despite bouts of homesickness, she thrived on her new life in Manhattan. New York was the focus of intense excitement among American poets, who were just then beginning to depart from traditional poetic forms and experiment with new, bolder, freer poetry. Millay was soon caught up not just in her courses, but in the city's literary society.

Everybody wanted to meet the author of "Renascence." She was invited to countless teas, lunches, and literary parties. Sara Teasdale, only 28 but already a celebrated poet, asked Millay to come visit for afternoon tea. The two women became friends immediately and spent the rest of the day together, talking and dining and, in the evening, riding around New York on the open top of a double-decker bus. The Poetry Society of America held a special lunch in Millay's honor. She was asked to read "Renascence" aloud but was too shy to perform before so distinguished and sophisticated an audience. Witter Bynner, whom she had finally met in person that day, read the now-famous poem for her, while she listened quietly with the audience.

After a semester at Barnard—and a string of literary and social triumphs—Millay returned to Camden, where she spent the summer in final preparations for the Vassar entrance examinations. Now that she knew she had a choice, she could live at home without feeling stifled or trapped. And she had friends now—poets, critics, and scholars throughout America—who understood and valued what she had to say. It was wonderful to be back on the Maine coast, within sight of gulls, meadows, orchards, and the magnificent mountains to the west and north.

"Renascence" had truly caused a rebirth for Millay: a reawakening of hope and ambition, and the start of a whole new life. If the future was a bit uncertain, that only made each day more exciting. "I don't know where I'm going," she wrote her mother, "but I'm on my way."

*Millay takes a stroll on the Vassar campus. Impatient with regulations, the independent young poet was often in trouble with college officials.*

# FOUR

# "This Pink-and-Gray College"

In the fall of 1913, Millay passed the difficult entrance examinations of Vassar College and joined its class of 1917. She was 21 when she entered Vassar, four years older than most of her classmates. During her time in New York, she had become part of the city's intellectual circles, respected as a serious poet by many prominent writers of the day. Since her early teens, she had handled both heavy responsibilities and an unusual degree of freedom. She considered herself an adult, as indeed she was.

Thus it came as a shock to discover that at Vassar she was expected to follow a long, detailed list of regulations, all designed for students far less mature and independent than she. Vassar women were required to attend chapel every day. Men could visit only on Sundays, and then only under strict supervision. Students were forbidden to miss class without an excuse, to leave school without written permission, even to walk across the campus late at night.

All these rules offended Millay. Soon after her arrival at Vassar, she sent a seething letter to Arthur Ficke, whom she addressed as "Dear Spiritual Adviser." Referring to the school colors, she wrote, "I hate this pink-and-gray college. If there had been a college in *Alice in Wonderland* it would be this college.... They treat us like an orphan asylum. They impose on us in a hundred ways and then bring on ice cream—and I hate ice cream. They trust us with everything but men—and

43

*For students of Millay's era, the Vassar Quadrangle (above) was off-limits at night, a restriction that profoundly irked the young woman from Maine.*

they let us see it, so it's worse than not trusting us at all." Vassar, she concluded, was a "hellhole."

Luckily for Millay, there was more to Vassar than rules of propriety. Its rural setting, in Poughkeepsie, New York, satisfied her love of natural beauty; at the same time, it was close enough to New York City for occasional weekend visits. And Vassar was one of the finest women's colleges in the United States. Its faculty was superb, its curriculum rich and varied. Henry Noble Mac-Cracken, the dynamic young educator who became its president in 1914, had been "amazed," he said, to discover that in his opinion Vassar's quality of teaching was superior to that of Harvard or Yale. The students were talented and enormously energetic; as

MacCracken said, the college had an atmosphere of "creative gaiety."

Almost all Vassar students were involved in the performing or creative arts, especially music and drama. There were songs, often composed by students, for every occasion from weekday dinners to the elaborate annual festivals. There was singing at chapel, at meals, and in a dozen other formal and informal settings. Several plays and pageants—again, often written by students—were staged every year. Some of these student productions even attracted the notice of New York drama critics. The *Miscellany*, Vassar's magazine, was read and praised far beyond the confines of the college.

Millay, who did nothing by halves, was soon caught up in the excitement of her courses and the college's nonstop student activities. By the end of her first semester, her intense hostility to the school had turned into an equally intense loyalty, and she could write home that she was "crazy about the college." She even set out to secure a Vassar scholarship for her sister Kathleen. (The effort was successful; Kathleen entered Vassar the year after her sister's graduation.)

College gave Millay a new awareness of social issues. According to President MacCracken, the years between 1890 and 1915 were "the period of the crusader" at Vassar. Both a suffrage club and a socialist club were founded during Millay's sophomore year. Like Mac-Cracken, who took a public stand in favor of woman suffrage (the right to vote), Millay became a strong proponent of equal rights for women. She also came to care deeply about social justice, the plight of the poor, and the prospect of war in Europe.

Millay was especially impressed when suffragist Inez Milholland, a recent Vassar graduate and one of the few American women then practicing law, arrived on campus to give a speech. Called the "Amazon beauty" of the suffrage movement, the glamorous Milholland was known for her courage and flair for drama (she had recently ridden a white horse at the head of a woman suffrage parade); the Vassar undergraduates adored her. When she spoke of her suffrage work and her efforts on behalf of striking seamstresses and women laundry workers, Millay was filled with admiration. Af-

ter the speech, Millay and other students flocked around Milholland and her husband, Eugen Boissevain, who also supported women's rights. There is no record of what impression, if any, the handsome, athletic Dutch businessman made on Millay. Their first meeting gave no hint that he would one day become a powerful influence in her life.

Inez Milholland was to die tragically in 1916, just four years before American women finally won the right to vote in national elections. Millay ded-

*Vassar president Henry Noble MacCracken attends a school function with his wife. Annoyed with Millay at first, MacCracken later became her good friend.*

*Leading 30,000 demonstrators in 1912, Inez Milholland (on horseback) campaigns for women's right to vote. Millay, like most of her classmates, idolized the fiery suffragist.*

icated a sonnet to her memory; a few years later, as an established poet, she read the sonnet aloud at the unveiling of a statue honoring women's rights leaders. The poem concludes with a call to action, written as if in the dead woman's voice:

> Only my standard on a taken hill
> Can cheat the mildew and the red-
>   brown rust
> And make immortal my adventurous
>   will.
> Even now the silk is tugging at the
>   staff:
> Take up the song; forget the epitaph.

Although her awareness of feminism and other social issues deepened during her Vassar years, Millay's main preoccupations were her classes, her many school activities, and her poetry—although certainly not in that order. Poetry always came first, and Millay was in constant trouble with school authorities for missing a class, forgetting an assignment, or wandering off into the woods in the middle of the night while in the throes of composing a poem.

Millay's exasperated teachers often complained about her to President MacCracken, who would then be obliged to call her into his office. He dreaded these interviews, knowing she was likely to rant, weep, and storm out of the room. On one memorable office visit, she cried so hard and long that she had to borrow two handkerchiefs from him. (She later returned them to MacCracken's wife with a note that may have implied some remorse: "Tell him I washed and ironed them myself.")

Not all Millay's professors found her difficult. Among those who respected her both as a poet and a person was Latin instructor Elizabeth Hazelton Haight. "She made me feel that there was no barrier of age between us," Haight wrote later. The two women shared a love of Latin poets: It was Haight who helped Millay master the technique of the *eclogue* (a poem usually written as a dialogue) and other

*Woodcocks tend their newly hatched chicks. Like countless other bird-watchers, Millay was fascinated by the male woodcock's dramatic "courtship dance."*

verse forms first used by the ancient Greeks and Romans.

Millay and Haight also shared a love of nature. The two women often rambled together through the lovely Hudson Valley countryside, sometimes conversing in Latin or English, sometimes just listening to nature's sounds. On one occasion they decided to seek out a woodcock's nest in the hope of witnessing the male's "sky courtship dance." Teacher and student skipped dinner, camped out in a likely spot, and waited for the moon to rise.

After a long, silent evening, they heard the woodcock cry out and saw him fly straight into the sky, so high that he was lost in the dusk. "Then," Haight recalled, "as suddenly he fell madly back to earth with whirring wings and a high song." Millay never forgot the soaring woodcock with his "watery call"; the bird appears in at least two of her poems. Haight, too, remembered that evening for the rest of her life. In her memoir, "Vincent at Vassar," Haight compared the poet to the bird: "Each flew in ecstasy to heaven; each fell back to earth singing."

Although Latin was Millay's favorite foreign language, she also studied Greek, French, German, Italian, and Spanish. She enjoyed her foreign-language and English courses and did well in them, but she did less well in the required mathematics and science courses, which bored her. As MacCracken put it, her work was "sometimes extraordinarily good and sometimes extraordinarily bad." Her grades

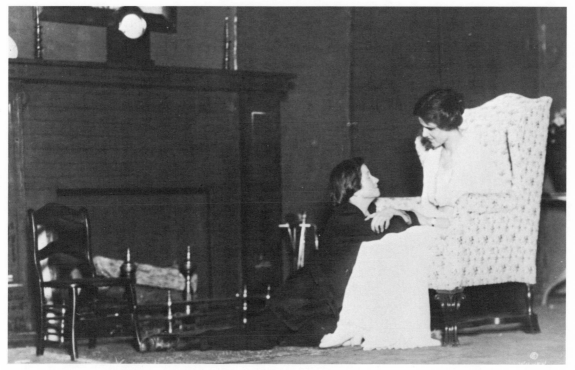

*A black-clad Millay plays the poet Marchbanks in Vassar's 1915 production of George Bernard Shaw's 1898 comedy,* Candida.

show, however, that the good work predominated. She managed to hold onto her scholarship, even though she refused to let schoolwork interfere with her poetry.

By the end of her sophomore year, Millay had won considerable praise for her acting skills. Her portrayal of the poet Marchbanks in George Bernard Shaw's *Candida* received excellent reviews from local and New York papers as well as from Vassar's own *Miscellany*. Junior and senior years brought even more acclaim. In 1916 she played the lead role in Irish playwright John Millington Synge's *Deir-*

*dre of the Sorrows*. One newspaper reviewer wrote of this performance that "Deirdre, small and bewitching . . . clinched the attention of the audience and the whole play."

Of all her Vassar acting roles, Millay considered that of Vigdis, the central character in a play called *The Locked Chest*, the most difficult and rewarding. Its author was John Masefield, one of England's most celebrated poets, and the Vassar production was the play's world premiere. Soon after her performance, Millay was thrilled to receive a letter from Masefield himself, who wrote that many friends had told him

*The students of Vassar College lived comfortably: Pictured here is a dormitory room furnished in the style of 1917, the year of Millay's graduation.*

what a fine job she had done in his new play. When he learned that the actress was also a poet, he invited her to send him some of her work and later wrote that he liked it very much. She had, he said, a "rare personal gift."

In her senior year at Vassar, Millay signed up for an experimental drama workshop and astonished her advisers by writing three plays during the course. One of them, *The Wall of*

*Dominoes*, a daring work about love and sexual passion, won first prize in a regional university competition and publication in the *Miscellany*. Another, *The Princess Marries the Page*, a light play that Millay thought "rather pretty," was produced at Vassar, with Millay in the leading role. It was later staged in New York and elsewhere. Both *The Princess Marries the Page* and Millay's third Vassar play, a blank-verse (unrhymed poetry) drama entitled *Two Slatterns and a King*, were published as books after Millay became an established writer.

Millay also took part in any number of school rituals. One of these, the Sophomore Tree Ceremony, a solemn occasion on which the class planted a tree for posterity, was almost entirely her own. She created a pageant, designed the written program, and wrote two songs for the 1915 event. The ceremony's central song was a plea for peace, probably a reaction to the specter of World War I, then raging in Europe and soon to involve the United States. Millay's classmates liked the Tree Ceremony so much that they voted to repeat it at graduation two years later.

During her college years Millay went on occasional double dates, and sometimes went out with Salomón de la Selva, a dashing Nicaraguan poet who had been her frequent escort while she was attending Barnard College. De la Selva was obviously smitten with Millay and her poems, and the couple had some wonderful times together. Most critics believe that "Recuerdo," one of Millay's most famous early poems, was written about him. In it she recalls a night when she and her friend, who were "very tired" but "very merry," went "back and forth all night" on the Staten Island ferry and "lay on a hilltop underneath the moon" until "the sun rose dripping, a bucketful of gold."

Although most of the poetry Millay wrote or revised during her Vassar years was first printed in college publications, she also sent her work to various national magazines. The distinguished *Poetry* magazine bought three of her poems in 1916, and Sara Teasdale included a Millay poem called "Ashes of Life" in an anthology of love poetry by women. One long poem by Millay, "The Suicide," won first place in an intercollegiate contest. This award gave Millay particular satisfaction because college officials had almost refused to let her submit it to the competition. The faculty committee reviewing Vassar's contest entries had been so shocked by the poem's subject that they never grasped the poet's meaning. Only when Millay appeared before the committee and read the poem aloud did the faculty members realize that it was clearly a cry *against* suicide.

Some of Millay's best poems of that era were written for college events. Among them was the "Baccalaureate Hymn," a song that became the centerpiece of the class's graduation exercises. The hymn, an imposing, rather somber work, begins:

> Thou great offended God of love and
> kindness,
> We have denied, we have forgotten
> Thee!
> With deafer sense endow, enlighten us
> with blindness, Who, having ears and
> eyes, nor hear nor see.

Everyone at Vassar agreed that the hymn was magnificent. But soon after she wrote it, Millay got into the worst scrape of her college career; because of

it, Vassar authorities barred her from attending the ceremony in which the hymn was sung, and very nearly prevented her from graduating with her class in June 1917. Her troubles had begun earlier that year, when she went to New York City for spring break. Offered a chance to hear legendary tenor Enrico Caruso sing at the Metropolitan Opera, the music-loving Millay was unable to resist, even though it meant returning to Vassar two days late. As a result, she was "campused"—forbidden to spend a night away from campus—for the remainder of the term.

For two months, Millay obeyed the restriction. Then, one sparkling May morning, she and her roommate joined two women friends for a ride in the friends' sports car. It was an exhilarating day to be out in the countryside on what was then called a "motor jaunt," and the young women lost track of time. They ended up spending the night at the home of one of the women's parents, a Baptist minister and his wife. On their way back to Vassar the next day, the group stopped for lunch at an inn, where Millay impulsively signed her name in the guest register.

The students managed to return to campus unobserved. But a few days later, a school official stopped for lunch at the inn and noticed Millay's name in the register. Aware that Millay had

*Millay (right center, wearing trailing white gown) takes part in the "Pageant of Athena" at Vassar's outdoor theater in the spring of 1915.*

*In Camden for the summer after her freshman year at Vassar, Millay (left) enjoys an outing with a friend from her grammar-school days.*

been campused, the official reported her discovery to the administration—some of whose members felt that Millay had already demonstrated intolerable disrespect for college rules. The authorities voted to suspend her from school indefinitely, which meant she could not graduate with her class.

To most students and many teachers, Millay's suspension was an outrage. Letters were written; petitions were circulated; meetings were called. Millay's supporters found it especially unjust that she should be barred from festivities largely based on her creations: the "Baccalaureate Hymn," the Tree Ceremony, the class marching song, and other poems and music. While the issue was under debate, Millay stayed in the off-campus home of the college physician, a loyal friend.

As it turned out, the administration was forced to allow Millay on campus for an hour a day to help the school choir rehearse the hymn, because nobody else knew the score well enough.

Finally, using the only veto of his career, President MacCracken overrode the faculty vote, but only in part: He ended Millay's suspension on graduation day itself, after most of the commencement ceremonies had already taken place. Millay was bitter about not getting to hear the hymn she had written, but she was immensely proud of her diploma. Shortly after graduation, she wrote to her sister Norma. "Tell Mother it is all right," she said. "I graduated in my cap & gown along with the rest." She signed her letter "Vincent (Edna St. Vincent Millay A.B.!)."

*Photographed during the period when she worked with the*
*Provincetown Players (1917–20), Millay models one of the flowing*
*gowns she wore for poetry readings.*

# FIVE

# The Village

Millay graduated from Vassar in June 1917. The following September, she moved to New York City, where she hoped to find work as an actress. Unsuccessful at first, she managed to earn some money by giving poetry readings. In a letter to her college roommate, she exulted about receiving "the fabulous sum of fifty dollars" for a reading. "It wasn't worth fifty cents," she said; "you know, I just sat in a chair and read [my poems] as I used to do for you kids. . . . Oh, my *God*, people are so good and kind to me!"

In December, Millay's sister Norma joined her in New York. At this time, most Americans considered it improper for young women to live alone without a parent or other chaperon. But in this as in most matters, the Millay women had little regard for social convention. Edna and Norma Millay set up

housekeeping in a drafty one-room apartment in Greenwich Village, a move that established them in their first real home away from home.

December 1917 also saw the publication of Millay's first book, *Renascence and Other Poems*. Slim and handsomely bound, the volume brought its author excellent reviews but no money. Nor did she earn any income from playing her first role on the New York stage. The theater group was the Provincetown Players, soon to be recognized as one of the most distinguished companies in the history of the American theater. The play's writer and director was Floyd Dell, an intellectual young editor, poet, novelist, and playwright from Davenport, Iowa.

Dell's play, *The Angel Intrudes*, included the role of Annabelle, a beautiful but flighty young woman. Because

*Floyd Dell (above, in 1930) fell in love with Millay as soon as he met her. She seemed, he wrote in his 1933 autobiography, "no mere mortal, but a goddess."*

none of the theater's resident members seemed right for the part, Dell issued a casting call. "In response to that call," Dell wrote later, came "a slender little girl with red-gold hair." This applicant, he continued, "looked her frivolous part to perfection and read the lines so winningly that she was at once engaged—at a salary of nothing at all, that being our artistic custom."

After her audition, the young actress wrote down her name and address and left the theater. "When she was gone we read the name and were puzzled," recalled Dell, "for it was 'Edna Millay.' We wondered if it could possibly be

Edna St. Vincent Millay, the author of that beautiful and astounding poem, 'Renascence.' "

He soon learned that the "slender little girl" was indeed the poet and that she was also a good actress (her performance as Annabelle, he said, was "delicious") and a gifted composer. For *Sweet-and-Twenty*, the next play Dell wrote and directed for the Provincetown Players, Millay composed the music for a song, which she herself sang. Dell later said he "fell in love with her voice at once; and with her spirit, when I came to know it, so full of indomitable courage." Like the many other men who became infatuated with Millay during her Greenwich Village days, Dell also stood in awe of her. "As a poet," he wrote, she seemed "no mere mortal, but a goddess; and though one could not but love her, he loved her hopelessly, as a goddess must be loved."

Millay was voted a full member of the Provincetown Players. Within a few months of her move to New York, she was thoroughly caught up in the tremendous energy of Greenwich Village. For several years preceding her arrival, young artists, writers, and intellectuals had flocked to the area, which most people simply called "the Village." It was a neighborhood of narrow, winding streets and old brick houses, innumerable bookshops, artists' studios, and small, inexpensive cafés and restaurants. In the Village a struggling artist or writer could live cheaply, away from the anonymous bustle of upper Manhattan. As more and more creative, independent young people moved there, the Village became a center of intellectual debate, artistic experimentation, and nontraditional life-styles.

During Millay's years there, the Village was probably more exciting, and its inhabitants more exuberantly productive, than at any time before or since. Millay threw herself into this new world with her usual fervor. To many of her friends and readers, she came to embody the spirit of the Village in the late teens and early 1920s: bold, bohemian, unconventional, and free.

With Floyd Dell, Millay explored the bistros and little theaters of the Village and came to know many of its more colorful inhabitants. The two writers became close friends, then began a love affair. Dell loved to listen while Millay read aloud: "Her reciting voice," he said, "had a loveliness that was heartbreakingly poignant." The pair spent their days writing or rehearsing and their nights acting, café hopping, or just racing through the Village streets, Millay's auburn hair flowing behind her and Dell in breathless pursuit. Millay and Dell—sometimes alone, sometimes with Norma and other companions—often sat up until dawn, passionately debating poetry, politics, and personalities.

Although Millay had written a few poems that touched on social issues and would soon complete an antiwar play, most of her work during this period was nonpolitical, dealing with such themes as love, death, God, and individual happiness. Nevertheless,

*A Greenwich Villager advertises the neighborhood's annual Halloween Ball. Like many artists and writers, Millay was attracted by the Village's freewheeling atmosphere.*

she shared many of Dell's then-radical views on pacifism, socialism, and feminism. She was, he would later write, "very much of a revolutionary in all her sympathies, and a whole-hearted feminist." And she deeply admired Dell's willingness to back up his political and social beliefs with words and action.

After the United States entered World War I in April 1917, Congress had passed the Sedition Act, which made it a crime to interfere with the war effort. In 1918, Dell and several other editors of the leftist magazine *The Masses* were arrested for publishing articles that protested America's entry into the war. Millay, who considered the arrest unjust, strongly supported Dell. She attended his trial and walked the courtroom halls with him, reciting poetry to distract him while he and his codefendants waited for the jury's verdict. After two trials, the accused editors were acquitted.

Dell and Millay could agree about poetry and politics, but they soon realized they agreed about little else. Millay firmly rejected Dell's frequent suggestions that she undergo psychoanalysis, as he had. As she put it in a poem written many years later, she had no desire to find "the lost and ominous key to the sealed chamber of my mind." Nevertheless, Dell kept on trying to delve into her psyche, hoping to discover her hidden thoughts and motives. Millay balked at this sort of probing. She also balked at Dell's proposal of marriage. The couple's romance, he later noted, "was haunted by her sense

*An unmarked gate guards the entrance to Chumley's, a Village speakeasy (illegal bar) often frequented by Millay. The café, now legal, is still in operation.*

of the inevitable impermanence of love. She refused to marry me. We parted several times." One aspect of Millay's attitude toward Dell is illustrated in her poem, "Travel," which concludes:

My heart is warm with the friends I
  make,
And better friends I'll not be knowing;
Yet there isn't a train I wouldn't take,
No matter where it's going.

Millay would probably have been reluctant to marry anyone at this time in her life. She was just starting out in her career and only beginning to explore the wider world. Dell wanted a conventional marriage, with children and a fairly predictable home life, while Millay hated the idea of being "domestic as a plate," as she put it. Such an existence, she believed, could stifle her talent or sap her creative energy. Not long after Millay and Dell finally agreed to part, Dell married a young woman of a more domestic temperament than Millay's. He and the poet, however, remained on friendly terms long after each had formed new romantic attachments.

Meanwhile, Millay continued her struggle to make ends meet, often shivering in her unheated apartment because sticks of firewood, at 10 cents apiece, were beyond her means. *Poetry* magazine editor Harriet Monroe had accepted five Millay poems for publication in June 1918; early in the year Millay wrote Monroe a half-serious note. "I could be very happy," she said, "except that I am broke. Would you mind paying me *now* instead of on publication for those so stunning verses of mine which you have?" Signing the letter "Wistfully yours," Millay added a postscript: "P.S. I am *awfully* broke. Would you mind paying me a lot?"

Millay may have been short of money, but she had more than enough suitors. Both as poet and personality, she was idolized by the young men of the Village. One of them, critic and essayist Edmund Wilson, later de-

*Literary critic Edmund Wilson (pictured in the 1940s) was among Millay's many admirers. Falling in love with her, he said, was an "inevitable consequence of knowing her."*

scribed her at the time: "She was one of those women whose features are not perfect ... but who, excited by the blood or the spirit, become almost supernaturally beautiful. She was small, but her figure was full, though she did not appear plump. She had a lovely and very long throat that gave her the look of a muse [a Greek goddess of art]."

Wilson said that falling in love with Millay was an "almost inevitable consequence of knowing her in those days." It was impossible, he added, to consider her poetry "without bringing into the foreground of the picture her intoxicating effect on people, because this so much created the atmosphere in which she composed." Although much of the poetry Millay wrote during her Village years concerns romantic love, none of her many admirers won her whole heart—until she met Arthur Ficke.

It was Arthur Davison Ficke who, along with his friend, Witter ("Hal") Bynner, had written Millay her first fan letter when "Renascence" appeared in 1912. She and Ficke had been exchanging letters ever since, but he lived in

*When poet and playwright Witter Bynner (above) asked Millay to marry him in 1921, she said, "If you really want me to, I will." She later changed her mind.*

Iowa, and she had never met him. In February 1918 Ficke appeared in New York City. Now a major in the U.S. Army, he was on his way to France with a packet of war dispatches for General John J. Pershing, commander of the American forces in Europe.

When he arrived in New York, the major asked his old friend Floyd Dell to introduce him to the author of "Renascence." This was easily arranged, and soon Dell, Ficke, Millay, her sister Norma, and Norma's fiancé were sitting on the floor of the Millay sisters' tiny apartment, trading witticisms and feasting on sandwiches and pickles, the most elaborate food they could afford.

Millay had long admired Ficke's poetic talent, which she believed the equal of her own, and his knowledge and critical judgment, which she thought far superior. When she finally met him in person, she was bowled over by his extraordinary good looks, athletic grace, and brilliant conversational ability. And to the rest of the group, it was obvious that Ficke was powerfully attracted to the witty, red-haired, green-eyed Millay.

Ficke was due to sail for France in a few days, but he and Millay made the most of their time together. Their brief, passionate interlude left Millay in what she described to Ficke as "a mist of thinking about you and writing sonnets to you." Looking back many years later, she recalled that she had been "terribly, sickeningly" in love with Ficke. The sonnets she wrote at this time, many of them probably addressed to Ficke, were magnificent, glowing with a new ro-

*Arthur Ficke embraces his wife, artist Gladys Brown (right), and Millay during a weekend visit from the poet. Millay, who met Ficke in 1918, became his lifelong friend.*

mantic energy. Here is one of the most masterful:

Into the golden vessel of great song
Let us pour all our passion; breast to
  breast
Let other lovers lie, in love and rest;
Not we,—articulate, so, but with the
  tongue
Of all the world: the churning blood,
  the long
Shuddering quiet, the desperate hot
  palms pressed
Sharply together upon the escaping
  guest,
The common soul, unguarded, and
  grown strong.
Longing alone is singer to the lute;
Let still on nettles in the open sigh
The minstrel, that in slumber is as
  mute
As any man, and love be far and high,
That else forsakes the topmost branch,
  a fruit
Found on the ground by every passer-
  by.

In this sonnet, and in her letters to Ficke, Millay maintains that passion itself, and especially the "great song" it engenders, is what counts, not love-making or even being together. "You are part of Loveliness to me," she wrote Ficke. "It doesn't matter that we never see each other." She undoubtedly meant what she said. But perhaps she was also putting a brave face on a heart-wrenching situation. She had no idea when, if ever, she would see Ficke again, now that he was off to war. And he was married; although he and his wife of 10 years had drifted far apart, she was chronically ill and he hesitated to divorce her.

That was the situation in 1918. After the war, it became clear that Ficke was not going to hasten to Millay's side at the first opportunity. Instead, he and Hal Bynner left on an extended tour of the Orient. In the end it was Bynner, not Ficke, who proposed marriage to Millay; she accepted without much enthusiasm, then changed her mind. And when Ficke finally divorced his wife, in the early 1920s, it was to marry another woman, a talented painter named Gladys Brown.

Millay, who made a special effort to befriend Brown, remained good friends with her former lover until his death some 25 years later. Although she never regretted her passion for him, she insisted she had not wanted to marry him. Nevertheless, his marriage must have been devastating to her at the time. It probably helped confirm the beliefs so often expressed in her poetry, that romantic love is fleeting by nature, and that lovers should accept this reality instead of deluding themselves with sentimental hypocrisy.

About two years after her older daughters moved to the Village, Cora Millay joined them in their new, slightly larger apartment. Soon afterward, Kathleen arrived. She had dropped out of college to try her hand at fiction writing (and, perhaps, to escape the long shadow cast by her famous sister at Vassar). The newcomers took to Village life with an enthusiasm that almost matched that of Edna Millay, who was delighted by their arrival.

Cora Millay was an immediate hit with her daughters' friends. Of all the Millay women, recalled Edmund Wilson, "it was the mother who was most extraordinary." Although she had "evidently been through a good deal," he said, she "had managed to remain very brisk and bright. She sat up straight and smoked cigarettes and quizzically followed the conversation. . . . She sometimes made remarks that were startling from the lips of a little old lady. But there was nothing sordid about her; you felt even more than with Edna that she had passed beyond . . . the power of hardship to worry her, and that she had attained there a certain gaiety."

Inhabited by four bright, spirited women, the Millay household became a kind of social and artistic center in Greenwich Village. Artists, painters, actors, writers, and social reformers would crowd the Millays' apartment, sitting at the feet of one daughter or another while Cora Millay looked on approvingly.

If the Millay family was as jaunty as it had been in Camden, it was also almost as poor; life in New York, even in the Village, cost far more than it did in Camden. In financial matters as in most things, the Millay women pooled their efforts. For a time, Norma did factory work and shared her modest wages with the family. Edna wrote steadily, but the market for poetry was limited, and even those magazines that published it paid very little.

To augment the family income, she began to write short stories and humorous sketches. Her prose pieces were readily accepted by the editors of such well-known magazines as *Vanity Fair* and *Ainslee's*, which paid more for fiction than they did for poetry. Because her first short story was scheduled to run in *Ainslee's* magazine in the same issue that carried one of her sonnets, Millay decided to sign it with a pen name: Nancy Boyd.

The income from the Nancy Boyd pieces was fairly steady, and it kept getting better. Millay could count on having *Ainslee's* magazine accept at least one submission every month, and by 1920, she was being paid as much as $400 per story. When she was running late for a deadline, Norma and Cora Millay sometimes collaborated with her, but only on the Boyd pieces; Edna St. Vincent Millay would never let anyone, even her editors, change so much as a comma in her "real writing."

Although Millay earned little from her poetry, her writing career progressed steadily. In 1920 *Reedy's Mirror*, a magazine that reached a large general audience, published a sequence of 20 Millay love sonnets. (A sonnet is a formally constructed, 14-line poem that usually expresses a single complete idea or sentiment.) This series helped confirm Millay's reputation as a technical master of traditional forms and proved that the sonnet—in her hands, at least—still had great poetic potential. But it was the content, more than the style, of these early sonnets that struck most readers.

Unlike most successful women poets

then writing, Millay avoided sentimentality. She did not pretend that passion could last forever. Nor did she shy away from the physical aspects of love. Perhaps most startling of all, she proclaimed that her work—poetry—was and should be more important to her than romantic love or lifelong attachment to any man. This idea of the openly passionate but fiercely independent young woman caught the mood of the Roaring Twenties, as the decade was often called.

Millay was also gaining a reputation as a playwright. One of her plays, *Aria da Capo*, reflected the spirit of the nation's rebellious youth as her sonnets had done, although for very different reasons. In structure, the action of the short verse play followed the *aria da capo*, a traditional, three-part operatic form whose first and third parts mirror each other. But the central themes of *Aria da Capo*—the pointless tragedy of war and the willful ignorance of humanity—were modern and timely.

*Elderly Germans search a Berlin garbage dump for food after World War I. The conflict's legacy of misery formed the theme of Millay's play* Aria da Capo.

*More than 8.5 million soldiers were killed in World War I. Millay's 1919 play,* Aria da Capo, *condemned the senseless carnage of war.*

At the end of Part 3, the frivolous, pleasure-seeking characters introduced in Part 1 sit at a banquet table. The audience can see what they cannot: corpses that have been shoved out of sight behind the tablecloth.

Far from making the world "safe for democracy," as its proponents had predicted it would, World War I had left a legacy of bitterness and hatred. *Aria da Capo* reflected the sense of disillusionment that afflicted much of America, particularly its younger generation, after the war. A huge and immediate success, the play, first staged in late 1919, was unanimously praised by theater critics: "The most beautiful and interesting play . . . now to be seen in

New York," said one. Another called it "a devastating indictment of man's folly," and a third described it as a "telling comment on human treachery and self-betrayal, which often nurture war because they ignore human need and human love."

*Aria da Capo* was staged all over the United States as well as in France. "I find myself suddenly famous," Millay wrote happily to a friend, "and in this unlooked-for excitement I find a stimulant that almost takes the place of booze!" Millay had no idea how much more famous she would become in the next few years or how her immense popularity would eventually complicate her life.

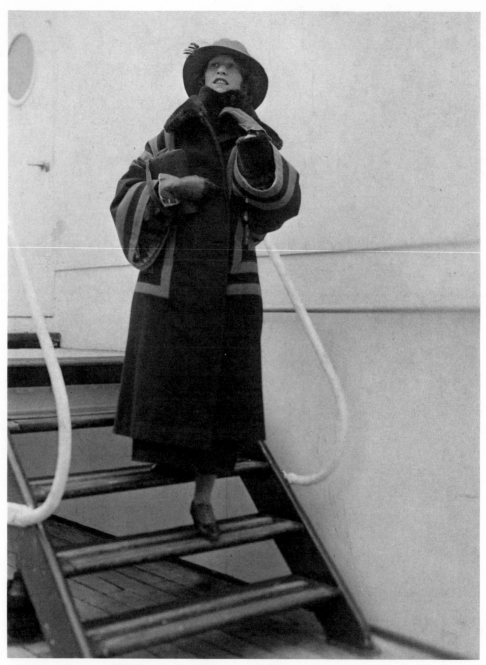

*After two years in Europe, Millay returns to America in 1923. While she was abroad, her third volume of poetry,* Second April, *was published to glowing reviews.*

# SIX

# "My Candle Burns at Both Ends"

During the early 1920s Millay worked and lived at an even more frantic pace than before. Between 1920 and 1923 she published three volumes of poetry, three plays, and several Nancy Boyd pieces. Although some of the poetry and two of the plays had been written earlier, each publication required extensive editing and polishing, tasks Millay undertook with her usual perfectionist zeal. Meanwhile, she continued to write both new poems and potboilers, the light, popular pieces that brought in needed income.

Her readers multiplied in 1920, when her work began to appear in fashionable *Vanity Fair* magazine and in the literary periodical *Reedy's Mirror*. Also in 1920, her second volume of poetry, *A Few Figs from Thistles*, was published. With its release, Millay's popularity took another leap, especially among the young, who felt that she spoke for them. *A Few Figs from Thistles* contains several short, metrically simple poems that were immediately memorized and recited by a host of college students and other members of the Jazz Age generation. The most popular of these poems was "First Fig," only four lines long:

> My candle burns at both ends;
> It will not last the night;
> But ah, my foes, and oh, my friends—
> It gives a lovely light!

The poet's message is clear: Seize the time, enjoy life while you can, live for the glorious moment. For Millay, of course, a life well lived included writing: The "lovely light" may have also

Vanity Fair *magazine proved a good market for Millay's work, much of which appeared under her pen name, Nancy Boyd.*

*Dancers demonstrate the Charleston— the most popular step of the Roaring Twenties—on a Chicago rooftop in 1926.*

referred to the poet's work. Whatever it stood for, it took the country by storm. "The First Fig," said literary commentator Vincent Sheean, "became a sort of motto or epigraph for the whole decade that followed it," a time, as he noted, of "careless wealth, crumbling standards, and deliberate revolt against society." Sheean called "First Fig" the "'Marseillaise' of that particular revolution." Equally pithy, even shorter, and almost as popular as the "candle" quatrain was "Second Fig":

Safe upon the solid rock the ugly
  houses stand:
Come and see my shining palace built
  upon the sand!

Among the other poems in *A Few Figs from Thistles* were several that stressed the transitory nature of love. Here is the first half of "Thursday":

And if I loved you Wednesday,
Well, what is that to you?
I do not love you Thursday—
So much is true.

Similarly, in "To the Not Impossible Him," the poet expresses her desire for wide romantic experience, even at the cost of fidelity.

How shall I know, unless I go
To Cairo and Cathay,
Whether or not this blessed spot
Is blest in every way?

Now it may be, the flower for me
Is this beneath my nose;
How shall I tell, unless I smell
The Carthaginian rose?

The fabric of my faithful love
No power shall dim or ravel
Whilst I stay here,—but oh, my dear,
If I should ever travel!

*A Few Figs from Thistles* established Millay as *the* poet of the Roaring Twenties. She was seen as a symbol of the "new woman," independent and sexually liberated. To men and women alike, she also represented the bold, rebellious, pleasure-loving, disillusioned youth of postwar America. She "captured the allegiance of her generation," says Millay biographer Norman A. Brittin, "exactly as J.D. Salinger [*The Catcher in the Rye*] for much the same reasons captured that of another postwar generation 30 years later." Millay's new book also excited readers outside the United States. The great English writer Thomas Hardy, author of such novels as *Tess of the d'Urbervilles*, remarked that America's two greatest assets were its modern architecture and its premier poet, Edna St. Vincent Millay.

But *A Few Figs* also drew some of Millay's harshest criticism in literary circles. Although some reviewers praised the book (one said it "let a gust of gay and impudent laughter in upon the feverish sentimentalism of the day"), most attacked it. Refusing to recognize the serious thought behind the book's light, witty tone, many critics condemned it as "merely cute," "shallowly cynical," or "pseudo-sophisticated."

Perhaps expecting such a reaction, Millay had planned to publish her more "serious" poems of this period in a

*Novelist J. D. Salinger (below), author of* The Catcher in the Rye *(1951), expressed the mood of his generation much as Millay's work reflected that of the Jazz Age.*

71

separate volume, to be released about the same time as *A Few Figs*. This collection, *Second April*, was ready for publication in the spring of 1920, but Millay's publisher, Mitchell Kennerly, ran into money problems. He did not publish *Second April* on schedule, and he refused to answer Millay's letters and telephone calls when she tried to protest the delay.

By 1920, Millay was an established poet, her reputation and popularity growing steadily. But just as she was being celebrated as the poet of *joie de vivre*, Millay found herself in a deeper depression than she had ever known. She was unhappy about Kennerly's foot-dragging, concerned that *A Few Figs*, appearing alone, created a false

*According to British writer Thomas Hardy (below), America's main contributions to the 1920s were modern architecture and Edna St. Vincent Millay.*

impression of her work. She was also distressed by a sudden decline in her health.

During her two years in New York, Millay had paid no attention to eating regular meals or getting enough sleep; she often stayed up for 24 hours at a time. "I'm strong as a pony," she had cheerfully boasted in 1918. Two years later, she was complaining of exhaustion. "I am so tired these days," she wrote to a friend, "working terribly, terribly hard." To another friend, she said she was "having a sort of nervous breakdown."

Even Manhattan had lost much of its charm for Millay. The Village had been "discovered" by tourists, and the city seemed increasingly noisy and frantic. A verse from "Eel-Grass," one of the poems in *Second April*, illustrates her mood at this time:

> No matter what I say,
> All that I really love
> Is the rain that flattens on the bay,
> And the eel-grass in the cove . . .

Deciding she might do better work with fewer distractions, Millay moved to her own apartment in 1920. But without her family as a buffer, she was "really besieged," as her friend Edmund Wilson put it, by the "importunities of her suitors." Soon after he met her, Wilson, then an editor of *Vanity Fair* magazine, joined the ranks of those suitors. (Another was Wilson's fellow *Vanity Fair* editor, poet John Peale Bishop. The magazine's top editor, recalled Wilson later, "complained that it was difficult to have both his assis-

# Poems by Edna St. Vincent Millay

*A New Set of Lyrics by the Most Distinguished American Poet of the Younger Generation*

## WILD SWANS

I LOOKED in my heart while the wild swans
 went over;—
And what did I see I had not seen before?
Only a question less or a question more;
Nothing to match the flight of wild birds flying.
Tiresome heart, forever living and dying!
House without air! I leave you and lock your
 door!
Wild swans, come over the town, come over
The town again, trailing your legs and crying!

## THE SINGIN' WOMAN FROM THE WOOD'S EDGE

WHAT should I be but a prophet and a liar
 Whose mother was a leprechaun, whose
 father was a friar?
Teethed on a crucifix and cradled under water,
What should I be but the fiend's god-daughter?

And who should be my playmates but the adder
 and the frog,
That was got beneath a furze-brush and born
 in a bog?
And what should be my singin', that was christened
 at an altar,
But *Aves* and *Credos* and psalms out of the
 psalter?

You will see such webs on the wet grass, maybe,
As a pixie-mother weaves for her baby;
You will find such flames at the wave's weedy ebb
As flashes in the meshes of a mermother's web.

But there comes to birth no common spawn
From the love of a priest for a leprechaun,
And you never have seen and you never will see
Such things as the things that swaddled me!

After all's said and after all's done,
What should I be but a harlot and a nun?

In through the bushes on any foggy day
My da would come a-swishin' of the drops away,
With a prayer for my death and a groan for my
 birth,
A-mumblin' of his beads for all that he was worth;

And there'd sit my ma with her knees beneath
 her chin,
A-lookin' in his face and a-drinkin' of it in,
And a-markin' in the moss some funny little sayin'
That would mean just the opposite of all that he
 was prayin'.

Oh, the things I haven't seen and the things I
 haven't known,
What with hedges and ditches till after I was
 grown,
And yanked both ways by my mother and my
 father,
With a *Which-would-you-better?* and a *Which-
would-you-rather?*

He taught me the holy talk of vesper and of matin,
He heard me my Greek and he heard me my
 Latin;
He blessed me and crossed me to keep my soul
 from evil,
And we watched him out of sight and we conjured
 up the devil!

With him for a sire and her for a dam,
What should I be but just what I am?

**EDNA ST. VINCENT MILLAY**

Edna St. Vincent Millay is one of the very few first-rate figures in modern American poetry. Her work, by the extraordinary vigor of its language and the sincerity of its emotion, achieves a lyric intensity scarcely to be found in the work of her contemporaries. Her best poems—and those printed here for the first time are some of her very best—have much more than the felicity of the artist contriving a literary form; they speak with the arresting naturalness and passion of a living human voice

## FOUR SONNETS

### I

WHEN you, that at this moment are to me
 Dearer than words on paper, shall depart,
And be no more the warder of my heart,
Whereof again myself shall hold the key;
And be no more—what now you seem to be—
The sun, from which all excellencies start
In a round nimbus, nor a broken dart
Of moonlight, even, splintered on the sea;

I shall remember only of this hour—
And weep somewhat, as now you see me weep—
The pathos of your love, that, like a flower,
Fearful of death yet amorous of sleep,
Droops for a moment and beholds, dismayed,
The wind whereon its petals shall be laid.

### II

HERE is a wound that never will heal, I know,
 Being wrought not of a dearness and a death,
But of a love turned ashes and the breath
Gone out of beauty; never again will grow
The grass on that scarred acre; though I sow
Young seed there yearly and the sky bequeath
Its friendly weathers down, far underneath
Shall be such bitterness of an old woe.

That April should be shattered by a gust,
That August should be levelled by a rain,
I can endure, and that the lifted dust
Of man should settle to the earth again;
But that a dream can die, will be a thrust
Between my ribs forever of hot pain.

### III

PITY me not because the light of day
 At close of day no longer walks the sky;
Pity me not for beauties passed away
From field and thicket as the year goes by;
Pity me not the waning of the moon,
Nor that the ebbing tide goes out to sea,
Nor that a man's desire is hushed so soon,
And you no longer look with love on me.

This have I known always: love is no more
Than the wide blossom which the wind assails,
Than the great tide that treads the shifting shore,
Strewing fresh wreckage gathered in the gales;
Pity me that the heart is slow to learn
What the swift mind beholds at every turn.

### IV

WHAT lips my lips have kissed, and where,
 and why,
I have forgotten, and what arms have lain
Under my head till morning; but the rain
Is full of ghosts tonight, that tap and sigh
Upon the glass and listen for reply,
And in my heart there stirs a quiet pain
For unremembered lads that not again
Will turn to me at midnight with a cry.

Thus in the winter stands the lonely tree,
Nor knows what birds have vanished one by one,
Yet knows its boughs more silent than before:
I cannot say what loves have come and gone,
I only know that summer sang in me
A little while, that in me sings no more.

## SPRING

TO what purpose, April, do you return again?
 Beauty is not enough.
You can no longer quiet me with the redness
Of little leaves opening stickily.
I know what I know.
The sun is hot on my neck as I observe
The spikes of the crocus.
The smell of the earth is good.
It is apparent that there is no death.
But what does that signify?
Not only under ground are the brains of men
Eaten by maggots.
Life in itself
Is nothing,
An empty cup, a flight of uncarpeted stairs.
It is not enough that yearly down this hill
April
Comes like an idiot, babbling and strewing flowers!

## WEEDS

WHITE with daisies and red with sorrel
 And empty, empty under the sky!
Life is a quest and love a quarrel—
Here is a place for me to lie.

Daisies spring from damnèd seeds,
 And this red fire that here I see
Is a worthless crop of crimson weeds,
 Cursed by farmers thriftily.

But here, unhated for an hour,
 The sorrel runs in ragged flame;
The daisy stands, a bastard flower,
 Like flowers that bear an honest name.

And here awhile, where no wind brings
 The baying of a pack athirst,
May sleep the sleep of blessed things,
 The blood too bright, the brow accurst.

*Calling Millay "the most distinguished American poet of the younger generation,"* Vanity Fair *ran a full page of her poetry in November 1920.*

73

tants in love with one of his most brilliant contributors.")

In the summer of 1920, Wilson visited the four Millay women in Cape Cod, Massachusetts, where they were living in a house borrowed from a friend. "I had never seen anything like this household," recalled Wilson later, "nor have I ever seen anything like it since." The house had no plumbing and almost no furniture, but the Millays, whose life-style had not changed much since their Camden days, seemed not to notice. They sang, they danced, they entertained Wilson with songs, and they sometimes even fed him. They were "rather vague about meals," but, he noted admiringly, "they never apologized for anything."

During this visit, Wilson, now "irretrievably in love" with Millay, asked her to marry him. She said she would think it over, but she did not sound very excited. To his dismay, Wilson thought he heard her whisper, "that might be the solution."

Millay loved Wilson after her fashion. Writing about their friendship in her superb poem, "Portrait," she says:

I could not ever nor can I to this day
Acquaint you with the triumph and
　　the sweet rest
These hours have brought to me and
　　always bring,—
Rapture, coloured like the wild bird's
　　neck and wing,
Comfort, softer than the feathers of its
　　breast.

But Wilson and Millay both came to agree that he was not "the solution,"

that she needed something more than the intellectual pleasures she shared with him. Instead of marrying Wilson or anyone else, she decided to travel to Europe. Wilson did not discourage her. Indeed, he coached her in French and helped her get assignments from *Vanity Fair* to report on the European scene.

In Europe, especially in France, Millay hoped to have "a change of everything"; as she told her mother, her poetry needed "fresh grass to feed on." She sailed for France on the steamer *Rochambeau* in January 1921. Characteristically, she refused to take any seasickness medicine on the voyage because, as she wrote her mother, she wanted "every bit of the experience," the good as well as the bad. When she arrived in Paris, she was almost penniless, but friends tided her over until she had finished some Nancy Boyd articles and stories for *Vanity Fair*. These pieces paid well enough for her to live—although very simply and with as many free meals as she could manage—for well over a year.

Except for one long poem, "The Ballad of the Harp-Weaver," which was inspired by her mother, Millay wrote little poetry in 1921. She spent most of her time editing and revising old work, sight-seeing, and socializing. She was enchanted with the beauty of Paris and the lively night life in its cafés and Left Bank jazz clubs. She went everywhere, soaking up the city's invigorating atmosphere and, despite occasional bouts of shyness, meeting new people.

In the summer of 1921, Millay's third

*Parisians enjoy a sunny day on the Champs-Elysées. Millay, who spoke excellent French, was enthralled by the sophisticated atmosphere of Paris.*

poetry collection, *Second April*, appeared in print. Among the book's selections were several poems written years earlier and revised many times. Although some reviewers commented that Millay's work often seemed to have been written almost effortlessly— an impression that complemented its clarity, grace, and directness—Millay worked very hard to achieve this "effortless" effect. She revised her poems endlessly, sometimes taking as long as 10 years to arrive at a version that satisfied her.

From its range, technical mastery, and depth of feeling and thought, *Second April* is clearly the work of a poet in her prime. The volume contains some of Millay's finest early love sonnets, several of them inspired by Arthur Ficke. It also includes the long, stun-

ning "Ode to Silence," which demonstrates Millay's unhappiness with the noisy world of New York. The other long poem in the volume, "The Poet and His Book," is among the best of the many poems Millay would write on the theme of death; here, the poet seeks to defeat it through her writing. "Read me," she implores the reader, "margin me with scrawling, / Do not let me die!"

In many ways, *Second April* is a sad book, the product of Millay's problems in New York and of a deeper disappointment with life and the world in general. Although some poems express a belief in the power of creative work and the beauty of nature, many others convey a sense of loss and despair. "To what purpose, April, do you return again?" the poet asks in "Spring," the

*Novelists F. Scott and Zelda Fitzgerald (above) were among the many expatriate American writers and artists Millay met in Paris.*

book's opening poem. "Beauty is not enough . . . . I know what I know."

*Second April* won raves from the critics. "If only I could sound a fanfare in words!" wrote the reviewer for *Poetry* magazine. "If I could get up on some high place and blow trumpets, and shout and wave my hands and throw my hat!" Millay, still in Paris, was delighted with the enthusiastic notices and with the publication that year of three of her plays, including *Aria da Capo.*

For Millay, the summer and fall of 1921 were happy seasons, with new

friendships and experiences and, it was rumored, a serious if short-lived love affair with a young Frenchman. In September, Millay went off on a round of travels, visiting Normandy with a group of writers and painters, then spending a few weeks in the English countryside and two months in Rome. She left the Italian capital to take a horseback journey through Albania and moved from there to Vienna, Austria. For the rest of the winter she stayed in Budapest, Hungary, where a group of American friends had taken up residence.

In Budapest, Millay received a $500 publisher's advance for a satirical novel she planned to write that spring. Vastly enthusiastic about the book, which she planned to entitle *Hardigut*, Millay promised her publisher it would be "amusing, satiric, ugly, beautiful, poetic, and an unmistakable allegory." As she outlined it, the novel would poke fun at conventional morality by portraying a society where food was a forbidden subject and eating before marriage considered immoral.

As soon as the advance check arrived, Millay began making plans for her mother to come to Paris. The prospect delighted her; she knew her mother had always yearned to travel, and she was proud to be the one to make it possible. "Not everybody," she said in a letter to her sister Norma, "can bring her mother to Europe." Millay had missed her mother terribly. In one of her many letters home, she wrote, "Mother, do you know, almost all people love their mothers, but I have never met anybody in my life, I think, who loved his mother as much as I love you."

Cora Millay arrived in France in April 1922. With her good humor and love of new experience, the bespectacled, gray-haired American was a great hit at parties and cafés. Millay found that seeing Paris through her mother's eyes made it even more appealing and gave her renewed hope and energy. But Millay's health was still quite poor— she had serious intestinal problems, aggravated by her sometimes heavy alcohol consumption and the food she had eaten during her travels.

In the summer, mother and daughter moved to Dorset, in rural England, where they lived quietly while Cora Millay practiced her nursing skills on her daughter. When Millay was well enough, the two women traveled to the south of France. There Millay hoped to write *Hardigut*, which she had told her publisher was almost ready for publication. In fact, however, she had written only the barest outline. She and her mother loved the south of France, but she found she had neither the inspiration nor the stamina to complete her novel.

In January 1923, after a brief trip to Italy, Millay and her mother returned to the United States. Settling into another tiny Greenwich Village apartment, Millay tried to write, but her work went badly: She composed few poems and soon gave up on *Hardigut*, her first and last attempt at writing a novel. By now, many of her friends had left New York for good. Her sisters

*Early 1923 found Millay in a deep depression, but the year would prove one of the happiest and most productive of the poet's life.*

were both married, and most of her old admirers, including Arthur Ficke, Floyd Dell, John Peale Bishop, and Edmund Wilson, had settled down with new wives or lovers. Approaching her 31st birthday, Millay was, she said only half-jokingly, almost "an old maid."

According to people who knew her during this period, Millay was ill and dispirited. Although she kept up a facade of enthusiasm and gaiety, she had few hopes for the immediate future. Coming events, however, were to prove her pessimism unfounded. The year 1923 would be one of the best in her life.

*Carrying her bridal bouquet, Millay faces the camera with her new husband, Eugen Jan Boissevain, soon after their July 1923 wedding in Croton-on-Hudson, New York.*

# SEVEN

# Settling Down, Branching Out

In the spring of 1923, a friend invited Millay to a house party in Croton-on-Hudson. A small riverbank town north of New York City, Croton had become, as one contemporary noted, "a kind of literary and political shrine"; it was now home to a number of writers and political activists from Millay's early Village days. Still tired, despondent, and ill, Millay declined the invitation at first, but the friend insisted and the poet finally agreed to go.

At the gathering were several familiar faces: Arthur Ficke and Floyd Dell and their wives, suffragist Doris Stevens, political writer Max Eastman, and Eugen Boissevain, widower of Millay's college hero, suffragist Inez Milholland. When the guests decided to stage an impromptu play, Millay found herself paired with Boissevain. The two had met at Vassar and again at a Greenwich Village party some years later, but neither had made much impression on the other. This time, however, something clicked.

Recalling the evening in his memoir, *Homecoming*, Floyd Dell wrote: "Eugen and Edna had the part of two lovers. . . . They acted their parts wonderfully, so remarkably, indeed, that it was apparent to us all that it wasn't just acting. We were having the unusual privilege of seeing a man and a girl fall in love with each other violently and in public, and telling each other so, and doing it very beautifully."

At 43, Boissevain was a tall, handsome man, endowed with what his friend Max Eastman called "the audac-

79

ity to enjoy the adventure of life." His "boisterous laughter," observed Joan Dash in her 1973 book, *A Life of One's Own*, "seemed to fill the rooms with the joy of living. Athletic, powerful, reckless as a pirate, he was also a singularly warmhearted man in whom strength was coupled with extraordinary sensitivity." The son of an Irish mother and a Dutch newspaper-owner father, Boissevain had traveled all over the world during his early years. He had hunted big game in Africa and

*Writer Max Eastman (below) said his friend Eugen Boissevain had "the genius, the audacity, and the uncompromising determination to enjoy the adventure of life."*

rowed in England's celebrated Henley Regatta.

After the death of Inez Milholland in 1916, Boissevain had entered the shipping business and eventually came to control a large fleet of merchant vessels and a flourishing coffee-importing company. Despite his success in business, Boissevain was drawn to the company of artists and other creative people; he was also a dedicated feminist. Outspoken and candid, Boissevain was immensely popular with women and men alike.

Millay sparkled during the play at Croton, but Boissevain realized she was not well and that the spirited house party had exhausted her. He took her to his home, called a doctor, and, reported Dell, "nursed her like a mother. His care at this time perhaps saved her life, for her condition, as shown by a subsequent operation, was very serious." The operation was major intestinal surgery, which Millay's doctors scheduled for July, some three months after the Croton party.

In May 1923, Millay wrote about Boissevain to her mother, who had returned to Maine. "You will like him very much when you know him, which will be soon," she said. "And it is important that you should like him,—because I love him very much, & am going to marry him. *There*!!!" Boissevain wanted the wedding to take place before Millay entered the hospital. That morning, July 18, with a few friends present and Millay attired in a white dress and veil, the couple was married at Boissevain's house in Croton. When the ceremony ended Boissevain rushed his bride to New York City, where she underwent surgery.

Many of Millay's friends, including Dell and Ficke, considered Boissevain the ideal husband for Millay. He was intelligent and romantic, but he was also fatherly, a protective bear of a man 12 years his wife's senior. And, unlike most of the other men who had courted Millay, Boissevain made no demands on her professional life. Rather than expecting her to curtail her writing so she could cook his meals and darn his socks, he eventually gave up his own career in order to further hers. "Anyone can buy and sell coffee," he once said, "but anyone cannot write poetry."

Several months after the wedding, Millay and her husband moved into their new home at 75½ Bedford Street in Greenwich Village. Three stories high, thirty feet deep, but only nine and one-half feet wide, the red brick structure was—and still is—the narrowest house in New York City. While Millay was recovering from her operation, Boissevain carefully guarded her privacy and her health; when she was writing or resting, he answered the telephone, coped with her stacks of mail, and acted as social secretary. He made sure that she ate regular meals, got plenty of sleep, and received the best of medical care. Meanwhile, she continued to work on her next poetry collection, *The Harp-Weaver and Other Poems*.

A rich, varied book, *The Harp-Weaver and Other Poems* is the product of mature vision and technical

*Nine and one-half feet wide, the Greenwich Village residence of Millay and her husband, Eugen Boissevain, remains New York City's narrowest house.*

mastery. All the old themes—romantic love, defiance of death, joy in beauty and nature, pride in artistic creation—are present, but they are subtler this time, more meditative. The book's title poem, "The Ballad of the Harp-Weaver," is a loving tribute to Cora Millay and the sacrifices she made for her children.

*Millay prepares to recite poetry on one of her cross-country tours.*
*Although she attracted standing-room-only crowds, she detested life*
*on the road.*

*The Harp-Weaver and Other Poems* also contains several of Millay's best-loved sonnets, some of which, for the first time in a Millay work, concern the prospect of growing old. Particularly popular with many readers is "What Lips My Lips Have Kissed":

What lips my lips have kissed, and
   where, and why,
I have forgotten, and what arms have
   lain
Under my head till morning; but the
   rain
Is full of ghosts tonight, that tap and
   sigh
Upon the glass and listen for reply,
And in my heart there stirs a quiet
   pain
For unremembered lads that not again
Will turn to me at midnight with a
   cry.
Thus in the winter stands the lonely
   tree,
Nor knows what birds have vanished
   one by one,
Yet knows its boughs more silent than
   before:
I cannot say what loves have come and
   gone,
I only know that summer sang in me
A little while, that in me sings no
   more.

Published in November 1923, *The Harp-Weaver and Other Poems* was greeted with a roar of critical and public acclaim. For the title poem, and for an expanded version of *A Few Figs from Thistles* and eight new sonnets published in 1922, Millay received America's most prestigious literary award: the Pulitzer Prize for poetry. The first woman to achieve this distinction, she was understandably excited by the honor: "If I die now, I shall be immortal!" she exulted to a friend.

The 1923 prize, along with the publication of *The Harp-Weaver and Other Poems*, solidly established Millay as America's leading lyric poet. "To most young people, according to *Time* magazine, 'poetry meant simply Edna St. Vincent Millay,'" notes Dash in *A Life of One's Own*. "She was read, quoted, copied, imitated, satirized, her comings and goings reported in gossip columns like a movie star's."

The Pulitzer Prize also brought an award of $1,000, the largest lump sum Millay had ever received. Writing to her mother about "my thousand bucks," she said, "I ain't going to bust [it] for god or hero—going to start a bank account with it." Millay's writing was finally starting to bring her a substantial income; with it, she began to pay off a series of debts she and her mother had incurred in Maine.

Millay was happy to be able to meet her obligations, but she was irked when others assumed all her money came from Boissevain. "I suppose it is a mean pride in me, but oh, I wish I could have done this before I got married!—because of course everybody thinks it is my rich husband who has done it, when in fact it is really I myself, every cent of it, with money I made by writing," she told her mother. Where personal and family expenses were concerned, Millay was determined to pay her own way.

It was largely for this reason that, in January 1924, she set out on a reading

*Millay and Boissevain relax on shipboard during their 1924 round-the-world tour. Stops on the trip included Japan, China, India, and France.*

tour of the Midwest. Millay was a stirring, dramatic reader. With her clear, lilting voice and flowing gowns, she won ovations from packed houses in Iowa, Illinois, and Wisconsin. But she hated almost every minute of the tour. She found the trains dirty and slow, the hotels uncomfortable and inefficient. She would, she told her husband, "sleep in the stock-yard" before she would ever return to Chicago's Windermere Hotel, which she called "the Goddamndest place I ever set an unwary foot in."

After a private reading for a group of wealthy Chicago admirers, she wrote Boissevain: "I kept saying over & over to myself while I was reading to them,

'Never mind—it's a hundred & fifty dollars.'—I hope I shall never write a poem again that more than five people will like." She missed her husband, and she longed for her literary and activist friends. Her health also suffered from the rigors of winter travel. Although she made several more tours during the next decade, she never really enjoyed them. Boissevain accompanied her on future tours, managing her schedule and strictly limiting her nonprofessional activities.

During the 1924 tour, Millay consoled herself by thinking about the prospect of an especially joyous spring. As a wedding present, Boissevain had offered Millay a trip to the Orient, which Millay had always longed to visit. "Oh, it will be so lovely when we go around the earth together!" she wrote him from the Midwest. In May the couple sailed from San Francisco to Hawaii, which Millay loved. "Eugen & I almost decided to leave the ship right there & spend the rest of our lives lying on the beach, playing duets on the ukulele & eating mangoes," she wrote her sister Norma.

From Hawaii, Millay and Boissevain traveled to Japan, China, Hong Kong, Java, Singapore, India, and France. It was a trip ideally suited to Millay's current needs: all the excitement of exotic places, but with the companionship of a loving, cosmopolitan husband and most of the comforts money could buy. Millay began to relax, and her health gradually improved.

Although the poet Edna St. Vincent Millay did not publish a new book in

1924, the light essayist Nancy Boyd did, producing her first and only anthology, *Distressing Dialogues*. Millay had steadfastly refused to sign the Boyd-style pieces with her real name, even when *Vanity Fair*'s editor had offered her more money to do so. Now, however, she decided to write—and sign—the preface for Boyd's book. She had fun doing it. Claiming to be "one of the author's earliest admirers," she recommended "these excellent small satires, from the pen of one in whose work I have a never-failing interest and delight."

Deciding they needed fresh air and more room than their tiny Village house offered, Millay and Boissevian started house hunting in the spring of 1925. They soon found a place that suited them perfectly, an upstate New York farm near the town of Austerlitz. Close to the Massachusetts state line, the 700-acre fruit-and-berry farm was situated in the foothills of the Berkshire mountains. The farmhouse was run down, but it was in a lovely spot and had dramatic mountain views and sloping meadows carpeted with wildflowers. And, to Millay's special delight, the farm was home to innumerable songbirds.

Because the hilltop farm abounded in wild steeplebush, a shrub that bears tall, pointed flowers, Millay named it Steepletop. She and Boissevain hired a small army of painters, carpenters, and

*Snow covers the countryside near Austerlitz, New York. Millay and Boissevain, who moved to this area in 1925, often enjoyed sleigh rides around their farm.*

*Surrounded by the cast of their 1927 opera,* The King's Henchman, *composer Deems Taylor and librettist Edna St. Vincent Millay take a bow on opening night.*

plumbers to renovate; Boissevain quit his importing business for good in order to run the house, oversee the farm, and free his wife for creative work. Steepletop would remain the couple's home for the rest of their lives.

Soon after Millay moved to Steepletop, Tufts University awarded her an honorary doctorate, the first of many such tributes she would receive over the next two decades. In the same year, after receiving a call from Deems Taylor, an old Paris friend, she began to work on an entirely new project. Tay-lor, a noted American composer and music critic, had been commissioned to write a new work for Manhattan's Metropolitan Opera Company. He asked Millay to write the libretto (the opera's story and lyrics). Thrilled by the opportunity to write the first American opera ever to be staged by the celebrated Met, she accepted his offer immediately.

For almost six months, Millay worked on a libretto based on the story of Snow White and the Seven Dwarfs. Often distracted by repairs at Steeple-

top and plagued by persistent head-
aches and spots before her eyes, she
found writing for the opera hard going.
But she was happy in her work, home,
and marriage, and her spirits and energy
were high.

Toward the end of the year, Millay
discarded the Snow White libretto and
started all over again, this time basing
her story on a ancient Anglo-Saxon tale
about a young man, best friend to a
king, who falls tragically in love with
the king's intended bride. As Millay
worked on through her first snowy winter at Steepletop, communicating with
Taylor only by mail, this version of the
opera began to fall into place. Finally,
at the end of 1926, words and music
were complete. The opera, entitled *The
King's Henchman*, was scheduled for
its opening performance at the Metropolitan Opera House on February 17,
1927.

The opera's premiere provided a brilliant evening and, by all accounts,
splendid performances by singers and
orchestra. When the curtain fell, Millay
and Taylor were called onstage for a
thunderous ovation from the enthusiastic audience. Critics hailed the work
as a great step forward for American
and English-language opera; the libretto, in particular, was praised for its
poetic beauty. Over the next few years

*A white picket fence guards Millay and
Boissevain's house at Steepletop. The
poet was enchanted by the area's
abundant wildlife.*

*The King's Henchman* was staged often, both in New York and in other
American cities. It was also published
as a play, without music, and sold
astonishingly well, going through some
18 printings in 9 months. Millay's fame
had reached even greater heights.

Despite the enormous success of the
*The King's Henchman*, Millay never
wrote another opera libretto, concen-
trating instead on her poetry. Safe in
her haven at Steepletop, working behind a sign ordering SILENCE, she
would write more than 10 full-length
books in about as many years.

*As Millay sat for this 1934 portrait by Charles Ellis (husband of her sister Norma), she composed "On Thought in Harness," a poem about a captive falcon.*

# Challenges

The late 1920s and early 1930s were good years for Millay and her husband: They were happy in their marriage, financially secure, and comfortable in their hilltop home. Millay produced an impressive body of work, and Boissevain found deep satisfaction in his role as manager of the farm and household. Although they were childless, neither appeared to regret it, perhaps because each had a substitute: Millay often spoke of her poems as "children," and Boissevain had established himself as the protector of his frail, younger wife, whom he sometimes called "my child."

Thanks to Millay's royalties and reading fees and Boissevain's income from his overseas investments, the couple had ample resources to run the farm and travel for part of each year. There were poetry-reading tours, visits to old

friends, excursions into New York for parties, theater, and opera, and long vacations, usually to such warm spots as Florida or the Caribbean, where Millay could swim.

Millay loved Steepletop, with its spring warblers, summer flowers and berries, fall foliage, and winter excursions by horse-drawn sleigh. She was surrounded by animals: Cows, sheep, and horses grazed in the meadows, herds of deer roamed the surrounding woodlands, and birds gathered everywhere. Speaking about his wife, who often arose at first light to feed them, Boissevain once said, "she runs a hotel for birds."

But much as Millay and her husband enjoyed their home in the mountains, they missed the ocean. In 1933 they bought a second, even more remote, home for midsummer vacations: wild,

*Millay and her husband share a quiet moment near their backyard bird feeder at Steepletop. His wife, joked Boissevain, ran a "hotel for birds."*

50-acre Ragged Island, in Casco Bay, Maine. The island's one ramshackle house lacked plumbing and electricity, but neither Millay nor her husband cared. Writing to a friend about Ragged Island, Boissevain called it "inaccessible, inhospitable and all together too wonderful and beautiful for words."

The couple spent long summer days on the beach or the rocks; when the sun was low in the sky, they dined on the day's catch of fish or lobster, washed down with wine. Millay sometimes spent whole afternoons floating in the salt water, mentally composing poems or just letting her mind drift with the sea currents. "She was part mermaid, apparently," wrote Vincent

Sheean, one of the few friends invited to the island. "[She] was quite insensible to cold or to fatigue in water; she always swam naked, and her love for the sea was as simple and direct as the love of the lark for the sky."

Whether at Ragged Island or Steepletop, Millay led a rather isolated life, but when her sense of justice was offended, she emerged from her cocoon quickly. In the spring of 1927, for example, she learned that the prestigious League of American Penwomen had expelled her dear friend, poet Elinor Wylie, for elop-

*When the League of American Penwomen expelled poet Elinor Wylie (below), a furious Millay joined her friend in "brilliant exile" from the organization.*

*Italian immigrants Bartolomeo Vanzetti (left) and Nicola Sacco await the outcome of their trial for killing two men during a 1920 payroll robbery.*

ing with a man she had not yet married. Outraged by the league's action, Millay fired off a furious letter. She would not even consider attending the league's upcoming writers' conference, she said, let alone accept its invitation to be guest of honor. "Believe me," she wrote, "if the eminent object of your pusillanimous [cowardly] attack has not directed her movements in conformity with your timid philosophies, no more have I mine. . . . Strike me too from your lists, and permit me, I beg you, to share with Elinor Wylie a brilliant exile from your fusty province."

That summer Millay again raised her voice in protest. This time, it was in defense of Nicola Sacco and Bartolomeo Vanzetti, poor Italian immigrants who had been convicted of robbery and murder in Massachusetts. The two men had been condemned to death—not, many believed, because they had been proved guilty, but because they were radicals and foreigners. The Sacco-Vanzetti case created an international furor; people of all political persuasions cried out against what they saw as a perversion of American justice.

As hopes for Sacco and Vanzetti's lives grew dimmer, Millay began writing impassioned letters and poetry. One of the poems, "Justice Denied in Massachusetts," asserts that the nation has cursed its future by betraying its own ideals. To their "children's children," she says, Americans will be leaving nothing but "a blighted earth to till / With a broken hoe."

Although Millay had recently been ill, she and Boissevain traveled to Boston, where they marched through the city the day before Sacco and Vanzetti were scheduled to die in the electric chair. The poet carried a large placard inscribed, "If these men are executed, justice is dead in Massachusetts." When Millay, who headed the column of protesters, was arrested for "loitering," Boissevain stood bail for her and several other detained activists. Later that day Millay read her poetry to a somber crowd; afterward, she met with the Massachusetts governor to beg him to delay the execution.

Despite the efforts of Millay and thousands of other concerned citizens, Sacco and Vanzetti were electrocuted at midnight on August 23, 1927. Sick and bitter, Millay returned to Steepletop with Boissevain; later in the year, she returned to Boston for her trial. Found guilty and fined $10 each, she and five other "loiterers," all of whom insisted on their right to speak and assemble peaceably, appealed the judgment. They were eventually acquitted, but for months afterward, Millay received stacks of mail accusing her of being a Communist and of spreading "vicious, false, wicked" lies in her defense of the condemned radicals.

"Justice Denied in Massachusetts" appeared in Millay's next volume of poetry, *The Buck in the Snow*, published in 1928. The volume contains some of Millay's finest poems; among them is the celebrated sonnet, "On Hearing a Symphony of Beethoven," which begins:

> Sweet sounds, oh, beautiful music, do not cease!
> Reject me not into the world again.
> With you alone is excellence and peace,
> Mankind made plausible, his purpose plain.

Against a world that seems ever more unreasonable and oppressive, says the poet, music is "my rampart, and my only one."

Between 1929 and 1939, Millay's output was prodigious. It included three volumes of adult poetry: *Fatal Interview* (1931), *Wine from These Grapes* (1934), and *Huntsman, What Quarry?* (1939). In 1929, she published a children's collection, *Poems Selected for Young People*; in 1932, a newly edited version of her Vassar play, *The Princess Marries the Page*; in 1936, a translation of *Les Fleurs du mal* (The flowers of evil) by the 19th-century French poet Charles Baudelaire, on which she collaborated with American poet George Dillon; and in 1937, a long dramatic poem entitled *Conversation at Midnight*.

*Fatal Interview* and *Wine from These Grapes*, the two poetry volumes that

*Arrested for protesting the 1927 death sentences of convicted murderers Sacco and Vanzetti, Millay (left) and a colleague head for jail with a Boston marshal.*

followed *The Buck in the Snow*, share with it a mature, contemplative attitude, in sharp contrast to the feverish ardor and the bold, almost impudent gaiety of some of Millay's early works. The wonder and fleeting nature of romantic love remain Millay's themes, but the loss of love is no longer treated flippantly.

Death, too, became harder to dismiss with jokes and taunts. In December 1928, Millay's beloved friend, poet Elinor Wylie, died suddenly at the age of 43. Millay received the shocking news just as she was about to begin a poetry reading. Heartbroken, she gave way to her grief for only a few minutes, then went on stage and recited Wylie's poems instead of her own.

Later, writing to Wylie's husband, poet William Rose Benét, Millay urged Wylie's friends to concentrate on the joys she had brought them rather than on their own sorrow. She had been, said Millay, "so gay and splendid about tragic things, so comically serious about silly ones." Despite such counsel, Millay herself was hard hit by the loss of her friend. A poem dedicated to Wylie begins, "When I think of you / I die too."

Two winters later Millay suffered an even heavier blow: In February 1931, Cora Millay died unexpectedly. After a funeral service in Camden, attended by the three Millay sisters and their husbands, Edna had Cora's body brought to Steepletop for burial. She mourned her mother for the rest of her life. "It's a changed world," she said in a letter to a friend. "The presence of that absence is everywhere."

Although Millay's poems still had the message that life must be lived to the fullest, they began to reveal a new sense of the inescapable reality of death. As biographer Miriam Gurko notes, Millay's "defiant resentment and repudiation of death deepened in this later poetry into something subtler and more reflective." In "Moriturus," from *The Buck in the Snow*, she was as defiant as ever:

> Withstanding Death
> Till Life be gone,
> I shall treasure my breath,
> I shall linger on.

At the approach of death, insists the poet, "I shall put up a fight, I shall take it hard." But in "The Leaf and the Tree" from *Wine from These Grapes*, she finds consolation in the thought that life will continue even after her own death: "When will you learn, my self, to be / A dying leaf on a living tree?" Then, especially in the sonnet sequence "Epitaph for the Race of Man," the poet begins to wonder whether the tree itself—the human race—will continue. But despite the increasing solemnity of her later works, Millay never lost her wonder at the beauty of love, nature, and humankind itself.

Writing about the poet in 1952, Millay's friend Edmund Wilson said she spent her middle years "alternating between vigorously creative periods when she produced the firm-based strong-molded work that represented her full artistic maturity—*Fatal Interview* and 'Epitaph for the Race of Man'—and dreadful lapses into depression and helplessness that sometimes lasted for months." But although the poet had to overcome massive obstacles, she continued to produce extraordinary work.

*Fatal Interview* and "Epitaph for the Race of Man" (which was published in book form as the closing section of *Wine from These Grapes*) are both sonnet sequences. Many critics, Edmund Wilson among them, rate these poems among the finest Millay ever produced.

*Fatal Interview*'s 52 sonnets recount the progress of a love affair; it was probably an actual one, although Millay always refused to discuss any connections between her work and her life. The poems take the reader from the first pangs of love—"This beast that rends me in the sight of all / This love, this longing, this oblivious thing"—to the rapture of union, and on to parting, grief, resignation, and bittersweet regret. To be appreciated, the sequence should be read in its entirety. But a hint of the honesty and passion that characterize the sonnets may be found in the following lines from "Not in a Silver Casket Cool with Pearls":

Love in the open hand, no thing but
    that,
Ungemmed, unhidden, wishing not to
    hurt,
As one should bring you cowslips in a
    hat

Swung from the hand, or apples in her
    skirt,
I bring you, calling out as children do:
"Look what I have!—And these are all
    for you."

"Epitaph For the Race of Man" is a meditation on the fate of the planet earth. In this 18-sonnet series and the book that contains it, the poet's objective, philosophical side becomes an important, even dominant, aspect of her work. "Epitaph" questions the permanence of the human race. After outlining humanity's place in the course of time and the vastness of the universe, she considers some of the species' nobler traits, but the concluding poems describe humanity's ignorance and self-destructiveness, which she predicts will cause its downfall: "You shall achieve destruction where you stand, / In intimate conflict, at your brother's hand."

Always distressed by humanity's warlike tendencies, Millay had become a staunch pacifist in reaction to the senseless butchery of World War I. During the 1930s, she watched with alarm as fascist (repressive, dictatorial) leaders—Adolf Hitler in Germany, Benito Mussolini in Italy, and Francisco Franco in Spain—swept into power. Horrified by fascism and the prospect of its expansion, she switched from dedicated pacifism to wholehearted antifascism by the end of the decade. The United States, she told a reporter in 1941, had no choice but to offer the "sternest resistance" to the onrushing forces of Europe's dictators.

*Barcelona Loyalists prepare to battle fascist rebels during the Spanish civil war, a conflict that took more than 1 million lives between 1936 and 1939.*

*Nazi leader Adolf Hitler arrives at a fascist rally in Kiel, Germany. Passionately opposed to fascism, Millay began to write propaganda during World War II.*

Millay's increasing interest in political issues led her to write a book unlike anything else she had created. Part dramatic dialogue, part formal poetry, part free verse, *Conversation at Midnight* takes place in a Manhattan town house. There, a group of men spend an evening discussing the great issues of the day, from communism, fascism, and war, to God and the nature of love. The dialogue leads to no specific conclusions, but it reflects most of the varying current opinions about the world in the mid-1930s.

Millay worked on *Conversation at Midnight* for more than a year. In the spring of 1936, when it was almost completed, she and Boissevain decided to take a vacation at Sanibel Island in Florida. After checking into their hotel, they had their bags sent to their room, then went to the beach to gather seashells. A few minutes later, they looked back at the hotel and saw an inferno: A flash fire quickly burned the structure to the ground, destroying everything they had brought with them. Describing the calamity to a friend, Millay wrote, "All my luggage went, and an emerald ring I thought very handsome, and, of course, the entire manuscript of what was to have been my next book." Every word of *Conversation* was gone.

Trying her best to be philosophical about the loss ("Fortunately, I have a very good memory," she wrote a friend), Millay returned to Steepletop and began to reconstruct the book. She found she could recall the poems she had considered complete, but that reinventing the others made for "an exhausting and

nerve-wracking time." Although she finally published *Conversation* in 1937, she was never fully satisfied with it. Unfortunately, the nation's literary critics felt the same way. Some said the book featured the worst lines the poet had ever written; one reviewer even suggested that she should have taken the Sanibel Island fire as a warning from heaven and abandoned the project.

A car accident in the summer of 1936 added to Millay's troubles. Her husband, who was driving at the time, reported the incident to a friend: "When [the car took] a sharp turn . . . the door flew open and Edna was thrown out and rolled down the embankment. She had a big bump on her little red-head, scratches and bruises all over, and her right arm was all banged up so that she cannot play the piano or use the typewriter. . . . We are not

*A lighthouse overlooks the beach at Sanibel Island, Florida, site of the hotel fire that destroyed Millay's* Conversation at Midnight *manuscript in 1936.*

pleased with God, although he might have done worse."

As a result of the accident, Millay spent the next five years visiting numerous specialists and undergoing a series of excruciating nerve operations. During this period, she was often in pain so severe that she could not type, work in her garden, or even think straight, much less write poetry. Not until three years after the accident did she complete her next collection, *Huntsman, What Quarry?* Several of the volume's poems, notably "Czecho-Slovakia," expressed the author's anxiety about Europe, where the carnage of World War II had begun.

*Cast members play a scene from Millay's* Conversation at Midnight. *The Broadway dramatization of her 1937 book appeared in 1964, 14 years after its author's death.*

By 1940, Millay was passionately committed to the Allied cause and to the need for American war preparedness, and her work showed it. Her new poems more closely resembled propaganda than art, but she felt obliged to write them as a service to her country. She hoped the public would accept them as such, understanding that these pieces were written with a sense of urgency and would be, as she put it, "faulty and unpolished." Still, she was hesitant when Harper's, her publisher, proposed a hardcover edition of her war poems.

She asked her old friend Arthur Ficke for advice; he told her flatly not to publish. The problem, he said, was not so much that this poetry "was propaganda as that it was *bad* propaganda." But Harper's insisted on publishing and Millay finally consented. When the collection, *Make Bright the Arrows*, appeared in 1940, it was greeted by savage reviews: One critic called it "nothing but fancy doggerel"; another said it might have been written by "a lady octopus caught in a whirlpool." Millay was dismayed, but she resolved to continue writing poems for what she called "my poor, foolish, bewildered, beloved country."

After the United States entered the war in December 1941, Millay joined the Writers' War Board, a government agency created to produce wartime propaganda. Among the many poems, speeches, and radio dramas she wrote for the board was *The Murder of Lidice*, a long dramatic poem about the Nazi destruction of a Czechoslovakian vil-

*U.S. warships explode as Japanese bombers strike Pearl Harbor, Hawaii, on December 7, 1941. The surprise attack triggered America's entry into World War II.*

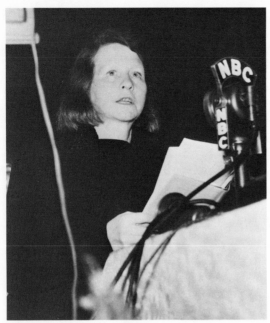

*A weary Millay acknowledges applause for her dramatic poem,* The Murder of Lidice, *in 1941. By this time, the poet's haggard appearance had begun to worry some of her old friends.*

lage. The poem was broadcast by radio across the United States and the Allied nations, with well-known actors and commentators reading the parts. At the end of the broadcast, Millay auctioned off the manuscript, which brought $1,000 for Czechoslovakian war relief.

Present in the broadcast studio were a number of Millay's old friends. Some, who had not seen her for years, were shocked by her appearance; ravaged by ongoing illness and constant pain, she looked frail and feverish. "She was a travesty of the girl I had known," wrote a woman who remembered Millay from her Greenwich Village days. "Her face

under the yellow thatch of hair had changed, almost unbelievably; it had aged but not ripened. With its flushed cheeks it reminded me of a wizened winter apple." Another old acquaintance said he thought Millay "looked like a stricken deer."

Millay had been beset by more than illness during the war years. She and her husband were consumed with worry about his family in Holland. After that country was overrun by Hitler's armies in 1940, the only news they had heard about Boissevain's relatives had been grim: A cousin had been tortured and killed by the Nazis. The war also led to the total collapse of Boissevain's fortune, which had been based on investments in Indonesia, a Dutch colony that had fallen to the Japanese. Boissevain and his wife now had to rely on her income, which had diminished sharply. The combination of wartime travel restrictions and her poor health halted Millay's well-paid poetry reading tours, and none of her work for the Writers' War Board was salaried. The publication of her *Collected Sonnets* (1941) and *Collected Lyrics* (1943) helped pay the medical and housekeeping bills, but money had become a worry.

Infinitely more distressing to Millay was the shocking news she received early in 1943: Her youngest sister, Kathleen, had died at the age of 46. A few months later, her editor at Harper's, whose advice and help she had relied on for 15 years, suffered a fatal heart attack. His death, she said, left her feeling "utterly lost."

In the summer of 1944, just as the war was nearing its end, Millay's strength gave out. Depressed after years of writing what she called "acres of bad poetry," demoralized by the heavy criticism it had drawn, saddened by the loss of people she loved, and exhausted by ongoing bouts of illness, she entered a New York City hospital. She had suffered what she later called "a very handsome—and, as I afterwards was told, an all but life-size—nervous breakdown."

Although Millay left the hospital after a few months, she was unable to write for the next two years. Writer Vincent Sheean, who visited her and Boissevain twice in the summer of 1945, reported that on the first occasion, she seemed "very frightened, small, and withdrawn." He said that although he had "previously described [her] as an astonishing beauty," at this meeting, she seemed "so small and mouselike that one imagined she might actually vanish at any moment."

But Millay was sometimes quite merry. When Sheean next saw her, two months later at Ragged Island, he said the poet "was glowing with health and spirits; her red hair was blown free and her green eyes were shining." During the visit, Millay recited some of her own work, thoroughly impressing Sheean. "She was a woman turned 50," he recalled, "dressed in rolled-up dungarees and a white sports shirt, and nevertheless she looked like a little girl of 12 at a party."

In the late 1940s Millay and Boissevain lived reclusively at Steepletop and Ragged Island. During these years, Millay became ever more dependent on Boissevain; he, in turn, became increasingly protective. As he always had, he answered the telephone, did most of the bookkeeping, shopping, cooking, and housework. And now, observes Jean Gould in her Millay biography, *The Poet and Her Book*, "he guarded her against unexpected callers or any interruptions like some huge, benevolent St. Bernard, gentle beneath his bark, but warding off unwelcome intruders."

Concerned about Millay's financial and emotional problems, her new editor at Harper's came up with several book ideas for her in 1948. The first was a collection of all her plays. Millay rejected it; only *Aria da Capo*, she said, was really good, and it was still in print. In that case, said the editor, what about a collection of Millay's love poetry? Each poem would be accompanied by a story about how—and to whom—it had been written. Millay needed money, but not that much. She was appalled by the idea of what she called "an erotic autobiography," and turned the project down instantly. She apologized for her refusals, asked her editor to be patient, and assured him new poems were in the works.

Indeed, Millay had begun to recover her spirits and start to write again. Working slowly at first, then with gathering momentum, by 1949 she had accumulated almost enough poetry for a new book. In June, she wrote a letter to her editor: "I have been working very hard, all day and during a great portion of the night also, for, I think, about seven months." In early August, replying to Edmund Wilson's letter suggesting a visit, she wrote, "This is awful; but I can't see you; I can't see anybody on earth just now; I am working 72 hours a day; and I don't dare run the risk of being deflected."

A few weeks later, just as Millay seemed to have regained command of her full creative powers, her world fell apart. In mid-August, Boissevain's doctor sent him to a Boston hospital to check out a persistent cough. The problem was quickly diagnosed: lung cancer. After the removal of his right lung, Boissevain appeared to be recovering, but on August 30, he suffered a fatal stroke.

Utterly stunned, Millay collapsed physically and emotionally. She spent several weeks in a New York hospital, then insisted on returning to Steepletop alone. Her friends were apprehensive about this plan. As her editor, Cass Canfield, later wrote, "There was a danger that in her melancholy condition she might commit suicide." But Millay prevailed and Canfield finally agreed to drive her to Steepletop. "When I left her in her lonely house," he recalled, "she thanked me for my detachment and said, 'I'm not going to kill myself. Don't worry.'"

The first winter after Boissevain's death was a time of solitary anguish for Millay; the first spring, with its happy memories of how her husband had loved the farm, was even worse in some ways. In an April letter to a friend, she said, "I have already encoun-

tered the first dandelion. I stood and stared at it with a kind of horror. . . . And suddenly, without my doing anything about it at all, my face just crumpled up and cried. How excited he always was when he saw the first dandelion!" But by the summer of 1950, she was beginning to recover, seeing people again, refurbishing her long-neglected house, and writing new poems for the book *Mine the Harvest*, which would be published in 1954.

For much of the summer, she worked on a Thanksgiving poem commissioned by the *Saturday Evening Post*. "Thanksgiving 1950" is a sober poem about cold war anxiety and the conflict in Korea. But it ends on a note of hope: "Let us turn for comfort to this simple fact: / We have been in trouble before . . . and we have come through."

The poem appeared as scheduled in November, but Millay never saw it in print. A month earlier, on October 18, she had stayed up until dawn, reading manuscript proofs. When the sun came up, she poured herself a glass of wine and started upstairs to bed. The following afternoon, October 19, her handyman found her sitting halfway up the stairs, her wineglass carefully set on the step above her. She was dead of a heart attack at the age of 58.

In his memoir, *The Indigo Bunting*, Vincent Sheean recalled the many conversations he had had with Millay about the birds she loved. His final conversation with her had been about the bunting, a small, brilliantly blue bird; her final, unfinished poem, he noted, concerned the same creature.

*The arrival of spring, 1950, in the Berkshire Hills (above) gave new strength to Millay, who had been despondent since the death of her husband in August 1949.*

The end of that fragment, found in her notebook, consists of three lines:

> I will control myself, or go inside.
> I will not flaw perfection with my
>   grief.
> Handsome, this day: no matter who
>   has died.

Because she was alone at the end, no one knew exactly what Millay's last activities were. But when Sheean learned she had been found "at the foot of the stairs leading to the poetry room" (her library-studio), he said, "I prefer to think she had been feeding the birds and was on her way to bed." It would come as no surprise, he said, to learn "that she died between the birds and the poets, for that is where she had lived."

A few days after Millay's death, relatives and close friends gathered at Steepletop for a simple memorial service. One friend played Beethoven's "Appassionata," one of Millay's favorite pieces of music. Her sister Norma, who was to make Steepletop into a colony for artists, read Millay's poem, "The Poet and His Book." Allan Ross Macdougall, who was to edit Millay's letters, read the poet's "Dirge Without Music," whose final stanza makes a fitting epitaph for its creator:

*Vincent Sheean works on a manuscript in the 1950s. His memoir,* The Indigo Bunting, *offered testimony to Millay's intense, lifelong love for birds.*

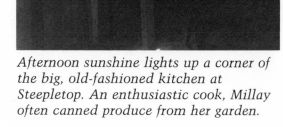

*Afternoon sunshine lights up a corner of the big, old-fashioned kitchen at Steepletop. An enthusiastic cook, Millay often canned produce from her garden.*

Down, down, down into the darkness
  of the grave
Gently they go, the beautiful, the ten-
  der, the kind;
Quietly they go, the intelligent, the
  witty, the brave.
I know. But I do not approve. And I am
  not resigned.

Until the mid-1930s, Millay was un-questionably the most popular poet in America, especially for the young. After the publication of *Make Bright the Arrows* in 1940, however, critics began to neglect or dismiss her work. Her propaganda writing had tarnished her reputation, to be sure; but the critics'

dissatisfaction went deeper. Millay's very popularity hurt her with some scholars and reviewers, and indeed with some readers. And the kind of poetry she wrote best—melodic, emotional, direct, fairly easy to understand—had gone out of fashion in postwar America.

Millay knew her poetry ran counter to the literary currents of the day, but she refused to let this knowledge affect the style of her later poems. She continued to test the limits of the sonnet form, and the years 1947–1949 saw the completion of some of her greatest sonnets. Her poetry in the posthumously

*The poetry of Edna St. Vincent Millay, seen here in one of her last photographs, proclaimed the value of individual human freedom.*

griefs among life's evils. . . . The whole volume has a 'sober coloring' that comes from maturity." In his 1982 study, *Edna St. Vincent Millay*, Brittin writes, "In an age of criticism and poetical dryness, the lyrical intensity of personal revelation in her poetry is striking. . . . Millay was responsible for destroying the restrictions upon women's expression and the prejudices against women's frankness." Her "constant theme," continues Brittin, "is devotion to freedom. The freedom of the individual, the freedom of woman completely to be an individual—these values engage her complete loyalty." *Mine the Harvest*, published four years after Millay's death, includes several poems that reflect that theme. One of them, "Not for a Nation," contains these lines:

> Not for the flag
> Of any land because myself was born
>     there
> Will I give up my life.
> But I will love that land where man is
>     free,
> And that will I defend.
> "To the end?" you ask, "To the
>     end?"—Naturally, to the end.

published *Mine the Harvest*, says literary critic Norman A. Brittin, "conveys the flavor of living in a world of wonders past and present, the endurance of

# FURTHER READING

Brittin, Norman A. *Edna St. Vincent Millay.* New York: Twayne, 1982.

Dash, Joan. *A Life of One's Own: Three Gifted Women and the Men They Married.* New York: Harper & Row, 1973.

Dell, Floyd. *Homecoming: An Autobiography.* New York: Farrar & Rinehart, 1933.

Eastman, Max. *Great Companions: Critical Memoirs of Some Famous Friends.* New York: Farrar, Straus and Cudahy, 1959.

Gould, Jean. *The Poet and Her Book: A Biography of Edna St. Vincent Millay.* New York: Dodd, Mead, 1969.

Gurko, Miriam. *Restless Spirit: The Life of Edna St. Vincent Millay.* New York: Crowell, 1962.

Millay, Edna St. Vincent. *Aria da Capo.* In *Twenty-Five Best Plays of the Modern American Theatre,* edited by John Gassner. New York: Crown, 1949.

———. *Collected Poems.* New York: Harper & Row, 1956.

———. *Conversation at Midnight.* New York: Harper & Brothers, 1937.

———. *The King's Henchman.* New York: Harper & Brothers, 1927.

———. *The Lamp and the Bell.* New York: Frank Shay, 1921.

———. *The Princess Marries the Page.* New York: Harper & Brothers, 1932.

———. *Two Slatterns and a King.* Cincinnati: Stewart Kidd, 1921.

Sheean, Vincent. *The Indigo Bunting: A Memoir of Edna St. Vincent Millay.* New York: Harper & Row, 1951.

Wilson, Edmund. *The Shores of Light: A Literary Chronicle of the Twenties and Thirties.* New York: Farrar, Straus and Young, 1952.

# CHRONOLOGY

| | |
|---|---|
| Feb. 22, 1892 | Edna St. Vincent Millay born in Rockland, Maine |
| 1900 | Parents divorce |
| 1909 | Millay graduates from high school in Camden, Maine |
| 1912 | Publishes her poem "Renascence" in *The Lyric Year*, a poetry anthology |
| 1913–17 | Attends Vassar College; graduates with A.B. degree |
| 1917 | Publishes *Renascence and Other Poems*; moves to Greenwich Village, New York; joins Provincetown Players |
| 1919 | Writes and directs a verse play, *Aria da Capo* |
| 1920 | Publishes poetry collection *A Few Figs from Thistles*; leaves for Europe |
| 1921 | Publishes two plays, *Two Slatterns and a King* and *The Lamp and Bell*, and publishes poetry collection *Second April* |
| 1923 | Returns to the United States; receives Pulitzer Prize for poetry; marries Eugen Boissevain; publishes *The Harp-Weaver and Other Poems* |
| 1924 | Takes world tour with Boissevain; publishes *Distressing Dialogues* under pseudonym Nancy Boyd |
| 1925 | With Boissevain, moves to Steepletop, a farm near Austerlitz, New York |
| 1927 | Completes libretto for an opera, *The King's Henchman*; joins protest movement opposing execution of Sacco and Vanzetti |
| 1928–32 | Publishes *The Buck in the Snow, Poems Selected for Young People, Fatal Interview*, and *The Princess Marries the Page* (a play) |
| 1933 | With Boissevain, buys Ragged Island, a vacation residence in Maine |
| 1934 | Publishes poetry collection *Wine from These Grapes* |
| 1936 | Publishes (with George Dillon) a translation of Baudelaire's *Flowers of Evil*; loses manuscript of new play, *Conversation at Midnight*, in a hotel fire; injured in car accident |
| 1937 | Publishes *Conversation at Midnight* |
| 1939 | Publishes poetry collection *Huntsman, What Quarry?* |
| 1940 | Begins writing war propaganda; publishes war-poetry collection, *Make Bright the Arrows* |
| 1942 | Publishes *The Murder of Lidice*, a long dramatic poem |
| 1944 | Suffers nervous breakdown; unable to write for two years |
| 1946–49 | Works on poems eventually published in *Mine the Harvest* (1954) |
| 1949 | Husband dies |
| Oct. 19, 1950 | Edna St. Vincent Millay dies of a heart attack at age 58 |

# INDEX

PICTURE CREDITS

The Beinecke Rare Book and Manuscript Library/Yale University, pp. 34, 63; The Bettmann Archive, pp. 32, 35, 37, 38, 39, 42, 46, 48, 59, 62, 66, 70 (right), 72, 75, 76, 80, 90 (right), 96, 99, 104 (left); Culver Pictures, pp. 12, 40, 61, 68, 84; Photos by Diana Gongora, pp. 60, 81; Impact Photos, p. 98; Lee County Visitor and Convention Bureau, p. 97; Maine Historical Preservation Commission, pp. 14–15, 18, 23, 26, 30–31, 33; Metropolitan Opera, p. 86; UPI/Bettmann Newsphotos, pp. 58, 71, 91, 93, 100, 105; *Vanity Fair*, pp. 70 (left), 73; Vassar College Library, pp. 2, 17, 19, 20, 22, 24, 27, 28, 44, 45, 49, 50, 52–53, 54, 56, 67, 77, 78, 82, 85, 87, 88, 90 (left), 103, 104 (right)

**Carolyn Daffron** is a writer and lawyer. A graduate of the University of Chicago and the Harvard Law School, she now lives in Philadelphia with her husband and young son.

❖   ❖   ❖

**Matina S. Horner** is president of Radcliffe College and associate professor of psychology and social relations at Harvard University. She is best known for her studies of women's motivation, achievement, and personality development. Dr. Horner serves on several national boards and advisory councils, including those of the National Science Foundation, Time Inc., and the Women's Research and Education Institute. She earned her B.A. from Bryn Mawr College and Ph.D. from the University of Michigan, and holds honorary degrees from many colleges and universities, including Mount Holyoke, Smith, Tufts, and the University of Pennsylvania.